SUPERSTARS
of the
WORLD
CUP

FRANCE 98

SUPERSTARS
of the
WORLD
CUP

Jon Palmer

P

·PARRAGON·

First published in Great Britain in 1998 by
Parragon
13 Whiteladies Road
Clifton
Bristol BS8 1PB

Hardback edition: ISBN 0-75252-418-6
Paperback edition: ISBN 0-75252-525-5

Produced by Prima Creative Services
Managing editor Tim Smith
Project editor Oliver Frey
Design and repro by Prima Creative Services

Printed and bound in Italy

Picture Acknowledgements

The publishers would like to thank Allsport, Action Images and Colorsport for their permission to reproduce the pictures in this book.
Allsport: 10, 11, 12, 68, 70, 71, 122, 126, 127, 168, 169, 204, 228, 228; Allsport MSI/Allsport: 8, 9, 94;
Allsport/Hulton Deutsch: 6, 9, 12, 94, 95, 228, 229; Allsport/Hulton-Getty: 7, 13; Allsport/Vandystadt: 77

ALLSPORT/Billy Stickland: 168; Patrick Bolger: 128, 209, 212, 252; Shaun Botterill: 38, 52, 79, 85, 91, 107, 108, 109, 119, 121, 132,
154, 166, 179, 182, 192, 195, 221, 231, 241, 242; Clive Brunskill: 20, 26, 39, 62, 103, 104, 105, 112, 133, 134, 138, 142, 143, 146,
147, 156, 157, 171, 177, 186, 187, 202, 203, 230, 254; Simon Bruty: 174, 176; David Cannon: 10, 11, 11, 22, 43, 94, 96, 153, 168,
191, 213, 214, 220, 222, 228; Graham Chadwick: 24, 46, 47, 111; Phil Cole: 45, 130, 188, 194, 226, 227, 234, 235, 238;
Michael Cooper: 63, 114, 117, 159; Jonathan Daniel: 129; Stephen Dunn: 198; Stu Forster: 31, 37, 54, 55, 59, 84, 102, 106, 113, 149,
152, 161, 189, 239, 248; Ross Kinnaird: 78, 170, 247; David Leah: 23, 88, 89, 160, 173, 197, 225, 211; Alex Livesy: 76, 185, 216;
Clive Mason: 48, 51, 58, 141, 148, 244; Steve Powell: 10; Gary M Prior: 82, 83, 140, 146, 193, 208; Ben Radford: 16, 17, 25, 29, 34,
35, 36, 50, 53, 56, 57, 60, 61, 69, 74, 75, 93, 100, 101, 110, 110, 116, 118, 124, 135, 145, 150, 151, 155, 158, 168, 172, 178, 180,
181, 184, 190, 199, 205, 218, 218, 219, 224, 240, 246, 249 , 255; Dave Rogers: 131; Mark Thompson, 28, 32, 40, 41, 64, 65, 67,
92, 120, 165, 167, 183, 200, 217, 236, 237, 250, 253; Martin Venegas: 97, 243; Claudio Villa: 198, 201; Anton Want: 245

ACTION IMAGES: 21, 33, 98, 99, 164, 175, 207

COLORSPORT: 12, 123

PUBLISHER'S NOTE

This book went to press on January 12th, 1998, and at that point the information contained within was held to be correct.
Only the footballing fates and managerial whims can be held responsible for any players included in these pages
not appearing in the World Cup finals.

SUPERSTARS
of the
WORLD CUP
CONTENTS

THE GROUPS

GROUP A
1. Brazil
2. Scotland
3. Morocco
4. Norway

GROUP B
1. Italy
2. Chile
3. Cameroon
4. Austria

GROUP C
1. France
2. South Africa
3. Saudi Arabia
4. Denmark

GROUP D
1. Spain
2. Nigeria
3. Paraguay
4. Bulgaria

GROUP E
1. Holland
2. Belgium
3. South Korea
4. Mexico

GROUP F
1. Germany
2. USA
3. Yugoslavia
4. Iran

GROUP G
1. Romania
2. Colombia
3. England
4. Tunisia

GROUP H
1. Argentina
2. Japan
3. Jamaica
4. Croatia

THE HISTORY OF A **Glorious**
68 YEARS

The World Cup is the planet's most important sporting event. An estimated television audience of 31.2 billion people watched USA 94. This topped the 26 billion people who watched Italia 90. FIFA now has 178 members – more than the United Nations – and over half the entire population of the world will watch football on TV as, for the second time in its 68-year history, the World Cup is staged in the country of its conception: France 98.

It was in Paris in 1904 that the idea of organizing a global football tournament was first properly conceived. Two Frenchmen, the President of La Fédération Internationale des Football Associations (FIFA) Jules Rimet and its official secretary Henri Delauney, can be credited with continuing that idea and, for over 20 years, running what has now become the world's greatest sporting event.

Jules Rimet in Uruguay, 1930

By 1928, professionalism meant that the Olympics were no longer a viable showcase for football at its highest level, and the inaugural World Cup was organized at last. Although Hungary, Italy, Holland, Spain and Sweden offered to host it, Uruguay, the Olympic champions, who were celebrating 100 years of independence in 1930, would host the first series.

URUGUAY 1930

Of the 41 members of FIFA, the Europeans balked at the three-week boat trip, even though a new stadium was built in Montevideo and the Uruguayans graciously offered to pay all travel expenses. Eventually, teams from France, Belgium, Yugoslavia and King Carol's personally selected Romanian XI made the trip, picking up the Brazilians on the way. The other competitors came from the Americas: Argentina, Paraguay, Peru, Chile, Mexico, Bolivia and the USA.

All the matches were played in Montevideo and the final was a repeat of the 1928 Olympic victory for Uruguay. The Jules Rimet trophy was awarded to José Nasazzi, and the Uruguayans took the following day off in celebration. Meanwhile, in Buenos Aires, the Uruguayan consulate was stormed in acrimony. World Cup football was born.

Goals Per Game: 3.89
Top Scorer: Stabile (Argentina) 8 goals
Final: *Uruguay 4–2 Argentina*
   Uruguay: Ballesteros, Nasazzi (captain), Mascheroni, Andrade, Fernandez, Gestido, Dorado 1, Scarone, Castro 1, Cea 1, Iriarte 1
   Argentina: Botasso, Della Torre, Paternoster, J Evaristo, Monti, Suarez, Peucelle 1, Varallo, Stabile 1, Ferreira (captain), M Evaristo

ITALY 1934

Still seething at the Europeans, Uruguay declined to attend, becoming the only World Cup champions not to defend their title. Despite their absence, 32 nations played off for places. At these early stages of the competition, the host nation was still forced to qualify, fortunately for FIFA, Italy managed it.

Of the 16 finalists, 12 were from Europe: Austria, Belgium, Czechoslovakia, France, Germany, Hungary, Italy, Holland, Romania, Spain, Sweden and Switzerland. These were joined by Egypt, the USA, Brazil, and by Argentina who brought a weakened team fearing defections to the Italians! Mexico were ordered to play a final qualifier against the USA which they lost, forcing a rapid return home. The knockout structure meant that the USA, who lost 7–1 to Italy, followed their southern neighbours back across the Atlantic after only one game.

The final was played on a smaller-than-regulation pitch where a late equalizer followed by an extra-time winner gave Mussolini's team their first World Cup.

Goals per game: 4.12
Top Scorers: Nejedly (Czechoslovakia),

1938's VILLAINS

The Italian team. Before the Norway game, the Italians repeated the fascist salute they had made in Rome four years earlier. Under orders, they held it until the jeers of the crowd subsided. Later, however, they were able to celebrate their win over Hungary.

Schiavio (Italy), Conen (Germany) 4
Final: *Italy 2–1 Czechoslovakia – aet*
  Italy: Combi (captain), Monzeglio, Allemandi, Ferraris IV, Monti, Bertolini, Guaita, Meazza, Schiavio 1, Ferrari, Orsi 1
  Czechoslovakia: Planicka (captain), Zenisek, Ctyroky, Kostalek, Cambal, Kreil, Junek, Svoboda, Sobotka, Nejedly, Puc 1

FRANCE 1938

The third World Cup was played amid the threat of war. The Austrians were forced to withdraw after the 1938 Nazi German 'Anschluss', while Argentina and Uruguay declined even to attend.

A change to the qualification rules meant that Italy as holders, and France as hosts, qualified automatically. They were joined by Belgium, Czechoslovakia, Germany, Hungary, Holland, Norway, Poland, Romania and Switzerland, with Brazil, Cuba and the Dutch East Indies the only non-European competitors.

The final was played as a contest between the brawn of the Italians and the skill of the Hungarians. Having taken a 3–1 half-time lead, the Italians were never troubled and won the trophy they were to keep for another 12 years.

Goals per game: 4.67
Top Scorer: Leonidas (Brazil) 8
Final: *Italy (3) 4–(1) 2 Hungary*
  Italy: Oliveiri, Foni, Rava, Serantoni, Andreolo, Locatelli, Biavati, Meazza (captain), Piola 2, Ferrari, Colaussi 2
  Hungary: Szabo, Polgar, Biro, Szalay, Szucs, Lazar, Sas, Vincze, Sarosi (captain) 1, Szengeller, Titkos 1

BRAZIL 1950

Possibly the strangest World Cup ever, Brazil 50 is the only tournament that ended without a final! However, as it turned out, the last game involved the only two teams who can won the final pool.

Little affected by the war, the Brazilians were chosen as hosts, and the famous Maracana stadium was built – well nearly – for the occasion. The Europeans were severely weakened and the Italians were further decimated by the Torino air-crash of 1949 that killed eight of their team.

The British Home Championship were designated a qualifying group, from which England and Scotland qualified. But the Scots stood by their decision not to go unless they won the Home Internationals. Portugal refused to take their place, while Turkey and India also withdrew. France offered to stand in but then too dropped out, leaving only 13 teams, the holders and hosts plus: Bolivia, Chile, England, Mexico, Paraguay, Spain, Sweden, Switzerland, USA, Uruguay and Yugoslavia. These travelled around Brazil to play, while the hosts contested five of their six matches in Rio.

A record crowd of 199,854 watched the Uruguayans reassert their dominance of world football at the Maracana, and the victory song the hopeful Brazilian hosts had composed for their team was never heard.

Goals per game: 4.00
Top Scorer: Ademir (Brazil) 9
Deciding Match: *Uruguay (0) 2–1 (0) Brazil*
  Uruguay: Maspoli, M Gonzalez, Tejera, Gambetta, Varela, Andrade, Ghiggia 1, Pérez, Míguez, Schiaffino 1, Morin
  Brazil: Barbosa, Augusto, Juvenal, Bauer, Danilo, Bigode, Friaca 1, Ziziho, Ademir, Jair, Chico

SWITZERLAND 1954

The World Cup continued to grow as 38 countries entered the qualifying competition to join Switzerland, Uruguay and hot favourites Hungary in the finals. England and Scotland both qualified, as did Austria, Belgium, Brazil, Czechoslovakia, France, Italy, Mexico, South Korea, Turkey, West Germany and Yugoslavia.

Hungary kicked off with 17 goals in two matches, beating South Korea 9–0 and West Germany 8–3. Sadly however, the most promising match of the tournament, Hungary v Brazil, degenerated into a riot as players and spectators fought on the pitch. The players later continued their quarrel in the dressing rooms in what became known as 'The Battle of Berne'.

But the biggest shock of all came in the final when Hungary were defeated by the unfancied West Germans. This was the Hungarian's first loss in 33 games spanning four years.

Goals per game: 5.38
Top Scorer: Kocsis (Hungary) 11
Final: *West Germany (2) 3–(2) 2 Hungary*
  West Germany: Turek, Posipal, Kohlmeyer, Eckel, Liebrich, Mai, Rahn 2,

Larry Gaetjens (USA), a Haitian by birth, he scored the goal that beat England in what was by then undoubtedly the greatest upset of all time. He sadly later dropped from view on his home island.

1950's VILLAIN

Rajko Mitic (Yugoslavia) – banged his head open on a girder and missed the start of the Brazil game. By the time he got on, Ademir had scored for the opposition.

1954's HERO

Ferenc Puskas (Hungary) – still suffering from an injury sustained earlier in the tournament, the greatest Hungarian player ever to play in the World Cup nearly tied the game for the 'Magic Magyars' with a late goal disallowed for off-side.

1954's VILLAIN

Gil Merrick (England) – a catalogue of goalkeeping errors helped Uruguay defeat England 4–2 despite having three players injured and no substitutes allowed to replace them.

1958's HERO

Just (pronounced Joost) Fontaine (France) – set a record of 13 goals in a single finals series that has never been beaten, though Gerd Mueller of West Germany scored a total of 14 in 1970 and 1974 combined.

1958's VILLAIN

Kurt Hamrin (Sweden) – played magnificently and scored as Sweden beat West Germany in the semi-finals, but he contrived to get Juskowiak sent off for retaliation.

1962's HERO

Garrincha (Brazil) – with lethal acceleration and the ability to shoot with either foot, the right-winger from Pau Grande transformed from the great player of Sweden 58 into the universally recognized star of this brilliant Brazilian side.

1962's VILLAIN

Ken Aston (England) – the referee failed to control the Chile v Italy game that saw one Italian get his nose broken and two more sent off. Giorgio Ferrini of Italy was made a scapegoat and was suspended for one match. It was eight minutes before the expelled player left the field.

1966's HERO

Bobby Charlton (England) – the inspiration behind the semi-final victory over Portugal that took England to Wembley. Charlton scored twice in a classic match of impeccable sportsmanship in which the first foul was not committed for 30 minutes.

1966's VILLAIN

Antonio Rattin (Argentina) – having had the better of the game, the captain possibly cost his side victory when he was sent off for dissent having already been booked in the quarter-final against England. He refused to go and it took a full ten minutes to get him off the pitch.

Morlock 1, O Walter, F Walter (captain), Schäfer

Hungary: Grosics, Buzansky, Lantos, Bozsik, Lorant, Zakarias, Czibor 1, Kocsis, Hidegkuti, Puskas (captain) 1, Toth

SWEDEN 1958

The first World Cup to be shown internationally on TV saw the beginning of the Brazilian's domination of world football.

The USSR entered for the first time, having invaded Hungary in 1956, some of whose leading players were caught abroad at the time and didn't play. The English team were depleted by the Munich air-crash but Wales and Northern Ireland qualified for the first time. Wales came through by default while Northern Ireland had to beat Italy 2–1 in Belfast. The Northern Irish team included Munich survivor Harry Gregg in their squad as goalkeeper. Both teams acquitted themselves well, reaching the quarter-finals of the tournament. The other qualifiers were Argentina, Austria, Czechoslovakia, France, Mexico, Paraguay, Scotland, West Germany and Yugoslavia.

Surprisingly, the hosts reached the final but were overwhelmed by a Brazilian team employing a revolutionary 4–2–4 formation. The Brazilian team included Didi, orchestrating from midfield, Garrincha on the right, with Vava and a 17-year-old prodigy called Pelé up front. Pelé announced his arrival by scoring twice, one an exquisite solo effort, to add to his hat-trick in the semi-finals.

Goals per game: 3.60
Top Scorer: Fontaine (France) 13
Final: *Brazil (2) 5–(1) 2 Sweden*
   Brazil: Gilmar, D Santos, N Santos, Zito, Bellini (captain), Orlando, Garrincha, Didi, Vava 2, Pelé 2, Zagalo 1
   Sweden: Svensson, Bergmark, Axbom, Boerjesson, Gustavsson, Parling, Hamrin, Gren, Simonsson 1, Liedholm (captain) 1, Skoglund

CHILE 1962

Although a series of earthquakes devastated the country in 1960, a plea to hold the World Cup was granted and a new national stadium was built in Santiago. Unfortunately for the hosts, their World Cup was to be the most ill tempered ever.

The qualifying nations were Argentina, Bulgaria, Colombia, Czechoslovakia, England, Italy, Hungary, Mexico, Spain, Switzerland, the USSR, Uruguay, West Germany and Yugoslavia. Violence in the first round caused the organizing committee to tell all 16 managers that such behaviour would not be tolerated. The threat proved hollow and the match between Chile and Italy was named 'The Battle of Santiago'.

After this disgraceful spectacle, Chile played well to fanatical support and won the third-place play-off. The Brazilians played a 4–3–3 formation known as 'the Penguin' – because it had no wings – and deserved their second successive victory, but the recurrent on-field violence spoilt the World Cup as a global celebration of football.

Goals per game: 2.78
Top Scorers: Garrincha, Vava (Brazil), L Sanchez (Chile), Jerkovic (Yugoslavia), Albert (Hungary), V Ivanov (USSR) 4
Final: *Brazil (1) 3 Czechoslovakia (1) 1*
   Brazil: Gilmar, D Santos, Mauro (captain), Zozimo, N Santos, Zito 1, Didi, Garrincha, Vava 1, Amarildo 1, Zagalo
   Czechoslovakia: Schroiff, Tichy, Novak (captain), Pluskal, Popluhar, Masopust 1, Pospichal, Scherer, Kvasniak, Kadraba, Jelinek

ENGLAND 1966

The nation that gave football to the world finally got its own World Cup. Argentina, Bulgaria, Chile, France, Hungary, Italy, Mexico, North Korea, Portugal, Spain, Switzerland, the USSR, Uruguay and eventual finalists West Germany joined the hosts and holders, Brazil, in England.

North Korea were the surprise team of the tournament, beating Italy 1–0 and then taking a 3–0 lead against Portugal before Eusebio scored four times to inspire the Portuguese to a 5–3 victory. The Portuguese then went out 2–1 to England in the semi-finals as West Germany beat the USSR by the same score.

In the final, the West Germans scored a late equalizer that took the game into a debilitating further 30 minutes. Controversy surrounded the extra-time goal awarded to the host nation by referee Gottfried Dienst and his linesman Tofik Bakhramov, who adjudged the ball to have crossed the line before bouncing out. Then with only seconds left to play, Geoff Hurst raced away to complete the only hat-trick ever scored in the final, and won the World Cup for Alf Ramsey's 'wingless wonders' as England had become known.

Goals per game: 2.78
Top Scorer: Eusebio (Portugal) 9

Referee Kreitlein counts to ten, as captain Antonio Rattin refuses to listen to reason.

Final: *England 4–2 West Germany – aet*
England: Banks, Cohen, Wilson, Stiles, J Charlton, Moore (captain), Ball, Hurst 3, Hunt, R Charlton, Peters 1
West Germany: Tilkowski, Hottges, Schulz, Weber 1, Schnellinger, Haller 1, Beckenbauer, Overath, Seeler (captain), Held, Emmerich

MEXICO 1970

A record 71 countries played the qualifiers in what was to become accepted as the best final tournament ever. Argentina were due to be hosts but FIFA decided their economy was too unstable and awarded the games to earthquake-stricken Mexico.

El Salvador qualified for the first time, even after their three qualifying matches against neighbours Honduras provoked 'the Football War'. The conflict, in which 3,000 people lost their lives, was actually the culmination of a long-term border dispute between the two countries.

South Korea were expelled after refusing to play Israel, who took their place. Belgium, Bulgaria, Czechoslovakia, Italy, Morocco, Peru, Romania, Sweden, Uruguay, the USSR and West Germany also travelled with the champions England, but no one could compete with Brazil.

With Pelé at his peak leading the line, Jairzinho's goals, Rivelino's ability to swerve the ball at will and Gerson's control of the mid-field, the Brazilians put on possibly the best football performance of all-time. This performance culminated with their devastation of Italy in the final which enabled them to claim the Jules Rimet trophy in perpetuity after a record third World Cup won.

Goals per game: 2.97
Top Scorer: Mueller (West Germany) 9
Final: *Brazil 4–1 Italy*
Brazil: Felix, Carlos Alberto (captain) 1, Brito, Piazza, Everaldo, Clodoaldo, Gerson 1, Jairzinho 1, Tostao, Pelé 1, Rivelino
Italy: Albertosi, Cera, Burgnich, Bertini (Juliano), Rosato, Facchetti (captain), Domenghini, Mazzola, De Sisti, Boninsegna 1 (Rivera), Riva

WEST GERMANY 1974

Following the tragic events at the Munich Olympics two years before, where terrorists had murdered several Israeli athletes, security was tight at this World Cup. The 74 finals were also notable for seemingly constant rain, and the players' growing fascination with big, big money.

Play-offs in qualifying were eliminated by the introduction of goal difference. Argentina, Australia, Bulgaria, Chile, East Germany, Haiti, Italy, Poland, Scotland, Sweden, Uruguay, Yugoslavia and Zaire came through, but it soon became clear that there were only two teams really able to compete for the ultimate prize.

Hero Beckenbauer lifts the Cup.

Although they didn't win, the tournament was lit up by Dutch 'Total Football'. Johan Cruyff's team changed positions to suit the moment, a tactic that bemused most of their opponents. The Dutch drew 0–0 with Sweden but beat their other opponents – including Brazil – comfortably to reach the final. The West Germans lost 1–0 to East Germany in their first and only encounter but won their other games to meet the Dutch in Munich.

In the final, the Dutch scored before the West Germans had even touched the ball after a surging run by Cruyff was unfairly stopped by Hoeness. The West Germans equalized from a dubious penalty, but the game was won when the instinctive Gerd Müller scored a typically opportunistic goal.

Goals per game: 2.55
Top Scorer: Lato (Poland) 7
Final: *West Germany 2–1 Holland*
West Germany: Maier, Beckenbauer (captain), Vogts, Schwarzenbeck, Breitner, Bonhof, Hoeness, Overath, Grabowsi, Müller, Holzenbein
Holland: Jongbloed, Suurbier, Rijsbergen (De Jong), Haan, Krol, Jansen, Neeskens, van Hanegem, Rep, Cruyff (captain), Rensenbrink, (R van de Kerkhof)

ARGENTINA 1978

The World Cup attracted 100 entrants for the first time. Iran and Tunisia made their debuts and were joined by Austria, Brazil, France, Hungary, Italy, Mexico, Holland, Peru, Poland, Scotland, Spain and Sweden.

A military coup in 1976 made Argentina a strange choice as host. But politics were the least of their opponents' worries as the host-nation exercized extreme gamesmanship. They even arranged to kick off their second-round match later than rivals Brazil, thereby knowing that a four-goal victory against Peru would see them through. Strangely, Peru's Argentinian-born goalkeeper Ramon Quiroga conceded six goals!

1978's HERO

Mario Kempes (Argentina) – the centre-forward proved himself the best striker in the competition by scoring twice in the final and setting up Bertoni for the third.

1978's VILLAIN

Willie Johnston (Scotland) – failed a dope test after his country's 3–1 defeat by Peru in their first game and was sent home in disgrace. The Scots were held 1–1 by Iran before recovering some pride by defeating the Dutch 3–2. They still went out after the first stage.

1982's HERO

Gerry Armstrong (Northern Ireland) – his first-half volley was enough to upset the hosts in the shock of the tournament. The result was even more remarkable after the questionable sending off of Mal Donaghy halfway through the second half.

1982's VILLAIN

Harald Schumacher (West Germany) – with the semi-final poised at France 1 West Germany 1, Patrick Battiston raced on to a through ball. Goalkeeper Schumacher came out to defend and brought him to the ground with a vicious forearm that knocked out two of his teeth and eliminated him from the game. No foul was given and Schumacher remained on the field.

1986's HERO

Diego Maradona (Argentina) – his brilliant individual effort against England in the quarter-finals remains one of the most remarkable moments of genius ever witnessed at this level. Very much the star of the tournament.

Mario Kempes – Argentina's saving grace.

The holders West Germany, now without Franz Beckenbauer, went out in the first round after failing to win a single game.

The entire tournament was riddled with poor refereeing, tactical fouls and violence. The final was a sorry affair that produced a foul for every 90 seconds of play, with the Dutch the main culprits. But it was the example set by the hosts that caused the bitter atmosphere in which the tournament was held.

Goals per game: 2.68
Top Scorer: Kempes (Argentina) 6
Final: *Argentina 3–1 Holland – aet*
  Argentina: Fillol, Olgu**ì**n, Galvan, Passarella (captain), Tarantini, Ard**ì**les (Larrosa), Gallego, Kempes 2, Bertoni 1, Luque, Ortiz (Houseman)
  Holland: Jongbloed, Krol (captain), Poortvliet, Brandts, Jansen, (Suurbier), W van de Kerkhof, Neeskens, Haan, Rep (Nanninga 1), Rensenbrink, R van de Kerkhof

SPAIN 1982

The number of teams was raised to 24, but the fixture list proved a failure as West Germany beat Austria 1–0 in a result that sent both sides through to the next round at the expense of Algeria.

Hungary beat El Salvador 10–1, while England and Brazil won all their opening games. The tournament structure showed more flaws in the second round as England went out after three wins, two draws and no defeats.

Italy kicked Maradona's Argentina into submission, but the Italian striker Paolo Rossi found his form to sink the favourites, Brazil. Then the Italians cruised past Poland in the semi-final. They met a resurgent West Germany in a disappointing final after the Germans played out a thrilling 3–3 semi-final with France before winning on penalties.

The other qualifiers were: Belgium, Cameroon, Chile, Czechoslovakia, Honduras, Kuwait, New Zealand, Northern Ireland, Peru, Scotland, the USSR and Yugoslavia.

Goals per game: 2.81

Top Scorer: Rossi (Italy) 6
Final: *Italy (0) 3–(0) 1 West Germany*
  Italy: Zoff (captain), Bergomi, Cabrini, Collovati, Scirea, Gentile, Oriale, Tardelli 1, Conti, Graziani (Altobelli 1, Causio), Rossi 1
  West Germany: Schumacher, Kaltz, K Forster, Stielike, B Forster, Breitner 1, Dremmler (Hrubesch), Littbarski, Briegel, Fischer (H Müller), Rummenigge (captain)

MEXICO 1986

Mexico became the first nation to host the finals twice, after Colombia withdrew, but a major earthquake the previous year made a nightmare of the already difficult task of organizing 52 matches in four weeks. Only eight teams were eliminated from the first round of 36 matches: Algeria, Canada, Hungary, Iraq, Northern Ireland, Portugal, Scotland and South Korea.

Argentina, Belgium, Brazil, Bulgaria, Denmark, England, France, Morocco, Paraguay, Poland, Spain, the USSR, Uruguay and West Germany all went into the knockout stages along with the holders and hosts. That these were the best finals since 1970 was testimony to the players. Matches were played at the hottest time of day to accommodate television, and the refereeing varied from inconsistent to slack.

The USSR demolished Hungary 6–0 before losing to surprise semi-finalists Belgium. Pat Jennings celebrated his 41st birthday with a record 119th cap for Northern Ireland, while Morocco topped their group only to find themselves up against West Germany in the second round. They lost to a late goal. France won the game of the tournament, putting out Brazil on penalties after an excellent quarter-final finished 1–1.

In all, three of the quarter-finals went to penalties but the best team eventually won under the guidance of Diego Maradona. He stole the show against England before

1986's VILLAIN

Diego Maradona (Argentina) – his brilliance was tarnished by the manner in which he achieved his first goal in the quarter-final against England. The referee was the only person in the world not to see the infamous 'Hand of God' incident, and Argentina won the match 2–1.

masterminding the defeats of Belgium and West Germany. Argentina took a two-goal lead at the Aztec stadium but were pegged back by West Germany until Burruchaga snatched a dramatic winner for them to deservedly secure their second World Cup trophy.

Goals per game: 2.54
Top Scorer: Lineker (England) 6
Final: *Argentina (1) 3–(0) 2 West Germany*
  Argentina: Pumpido, Cuciuffo, Olarticoechea, Ruggeri, Brown 1, Giusti, Burruchaga 1 (Trobbiani), Batista, Valdano 1, Maradona (captain), Enrique
  West Germany: Schumacher, Berthold, Briegel, Jakobs, Forster, Eder, Brehme, Matthäus, Allofs (Völler 1), Magath (D Hoeness), Rummenigge (captain) 1

ITALY 1990

This was a disappointing World Cup in which, with the exception of Paul Gascoigne, Gianluca Vialli and Roger Milla, few players made names for themselves. FIFA insisted on red cards for 'professional fouls' on the eve of the tournament which resulted in a record 164 bookings and 16 red cards – half of them in matches with the defending champions, Argentina.

It started well enough, with unfancied Cameroon defeating the holders with a Biyick goal and only nine men. The Africans then beat Romania 2–1, before defeating Colombia by the same score in the second phase. Cameroon provided much of the entertainment, but their cynical fouling, notably of Maradona and Cannigia in the first match, was their eventual downfall as they went out to two Gary Lineker penalties in the quarter-final against England.

Sadly, the tournament saw an unimaginative Argentinian team meet the equally dour West Germans in a final neither side deserved to be in. In this unsportsman-like game Argentina had two players sent off before losing to a highly dubious late penalty. FIFA's response to the world's disappointment was to introduce a rule in 1992 forbidding goalkeepers to handle back-passes.

Austria, Belgium, Brazil, Czechoslovakia, Egypt, Eire, Holland, South Korea, Spain, Sweden, the UAE, the USA, the USSR, Uruguay and Yugoslavia also competed.

Goals per game: 2.21
Top Scorer: Schillaci (Italy) 5
Final: *Germany (0) 1–(0) 0 Argentina*
  Germany: Illgner, Berthold (Reuter), Kohler, Augenthaler, Buchwald, Brehme 1 pen, Littbarski, Hässler, Matthäus (captain), Völler, Klinsmann
  Argentina: Goycochea, Lorenzo, Serrizuela, Sensini, Ruggeri (Monzon), Simon, Basualdo, Burruchaga (Calderon), Maradona (captain), Troglio, Dezotti

USA 1994

New disciplinary records were set amid new FIFA rulings and inconsistent refereeing. Brazil – still mourning the death of Ayrton Senna – won a record fourth World Cup to add another star to their crest. But the celebrations were soured when Colombian centre-back Andres Escobar was shot dead outside a bar in his hometown of Medellin a few days after scoring an own-goal in his country's 2–1 defeat by the hosts. Colombia, among the pre-tournament favourites, went home after the first round.

Belgium, Bulgaria, Cameroon, Eire, Holland, Germany, Greece, Italy, Mexico, Morocco, Nigeria, Norway, Romania, Russia, Saudi Arabia, South Korea, Spain, Sweden and Switzerland also entered as qualifiers.

The final was billed as the battle between Brazilian flair and Italian caution. In the event neither side showed any urge to attack, both waiting for a defensive error for the poacher Romario to latch onto or a moment of brilliance from Roberto Baggio. In the second period of extra-time, Baggio found himself unmarked in the penalty area with the ball at his feet, but Taffarel saved. After 120 minutes of goal-less football a penalty shoot-out separated the two finalists for the first time.

With the score at 2–2, Claudio Taffarel, the Brazilian goalkeeper and a practising Christian, dived to the left to save Massaro's shot before pointing towards the sky, committing the save to Jesus. Dunga, slated by the Brazilian press after Italia 90, stepped up to score. The Buddhist Roberto Baggio then sent his penalty over the bar and Brazil won the World Cup.

Goals per game: 2.71
Top Scorer: Salenko (Russia) 6
Final: *Brazil (0) 0–(0) 0 Italy – aet.*
    Brazil won 3–2 on penalties
  Brazil: Taffarel, Jorginho (Cafu), Aldair, Marcio Santos, Branco, Mazinho (Viola), Dunga (captain), Mauro Silva, Zinho, Romario, Bebeto
  Italy: Pagliuca, Mussi (Appoloni), Maldini, Baresi (captain), Benarrivo, Berti, Albertini, D Baggio (Evani), Donadoni, R Baggio, Massaro

FRANCE 1998

Even if the hype surrounding the last two World Cups has only produced disappointment, the world's most prestigious celebration of sport still continues to grow. For the first time ever France 98 will see no fewer than 32 nations competing. The eternal hope is that these finals will prove the best yet.

Here are some of the players I most expect to make this hope a reality.

—*Jon Palmer*

1990's HERO

Roger Milla (Cameroon) – nobody knew how old he was, though he was certainly at least 38, but he was the fire in the Cameroon team and his celebratory dances around the corner flags after each of his four goals will never be forgotten.

1990's VILLAIN

Rene Higuita (Colombia) – the flamboyant goalkeeper's recklessness cost his team the match against Cameroon. A full 40 yards out of his goal, he lost the ball to Roger Milla, who scored what proved to be the goal that put Colombia out.

1994's HERO

Romario (Brazil) – Despite the well-reported rift between himself and his striking partner Bebeto, he scored or had a hand in 10 of Brazil's 11 goals, was outstanding throughout and showed true team-spirit by joining in the dedication of one goal to Bebeto's new-born baby.

1994's VILLAIN

Diego Maradona (Argentina) – the beleaguered Argentine captain was expelled on failing a dope test after the 2–1 defeat of Nigeria. Traces of the banned substance ephedrine were found in his bloodstream and he watched the rest of the tournament from behind a pair of sunglasses.

NAME:
Just Fontaine

COUNTRY:
France

WORLD CUPS:
1958

The Moroccan-born striker's strength, speed and direct style was similar to that now shown by Brazil's Ronaldo (see page 71).

NAME:
Eusebio da Silva Ferreira

COUNTRY:
Portugal

WORLD CUPS:
1966

Such is the fame of this powerful Mozambiquean that his statue now dominates the entrance of Benfica's Estadio da Luz.

NAME:
Gerd Mueller

COUNTRY:
West Germany

WORLD CUPS:
1970, 1974

Powerful heading and the ability to turn on a sixpence helped this short and stocky man to a sensational 68 goals in 62 internationals.

NAME:
Paolo Rossi

COUNTRY:
Italy

WORLD CUPS:
1978, 1982

The star of two World Cups would surely have broken all World Cup goalscoring records had he not retired aged only 29.

NAME:
Diego Armando Maradona

COUNTRY:
Argentina

WORLD CUPS:
1982, 1986, 1990, 1994

Maradona's left foot was the finest ever but 'el pibe de oro' (the golden boy) is a victim of a world that expected too much from him.

TACTICAL INNOVATIONS

THE BRAZILANS
4-2-4

1958 was the year that saw Pelé's World Cup debut in a team that concentrated on attack. The salient point of their tactics was that Garrincha and Zagalo fed Vava and Pelé from the wings. Champions Brazil and England would drop the wingers in the 1960s, but Brazil would return to this formation in 1970 to produce attacking football at its best. They will be less adventurous in France with the wide players operating from deep in their own halves.

THE GREATEST

NAME:
Edson Arantes do Nascimento –
'Pelé'

COUNTRY:
Brazil

BORN:
21.10.40

BIRTHPLACE:
Tres Coracoes

WORLD CUPS:
1958, 1962, 1966, 1970

CAPS:
92 (77 goals)

MOMENT OF GLORY

Widely regarded as the greatest player ever to kick a ball, Pelé was born to a father whose own playing career barely earned a living and a mother who tried to discourage her son from following the same path in life. Pelé, however, says he was 'born for soccer, just as Beethoven was born for music', and as a child he would juggle melons whenever deprived of a real ball.

Although justly famed for his sportsmanship and heartfelt love of the game, there are incidents of fighting and dissent from his early playing career that the world prefers to forget. However, he was never sent off while playing abroad and at 17 he became the youngest player ever to receive a World Cup winner's medal. As he matured, his tempestuous streak was quelled and his football took over.

He played well over 1,000 top-class matches, averaging a goal a game, many for Santos, the club he served for most of his illustrious career. With the experience of four World Cups behind him, he has become the world's leading footballing ambassador, promoting his 'beautiful game' around the world, especially amongst the poor and underprivileged from whose ranks he emerged.

Wingers move forwards to become new attackers

ATTACK
Saudi Arabia
AL-JABER

Saudi Arabia's second successive World Cup qualification has been achieved with the help of an extremely pacy striker who broke into the team as the Saudis were claiming their place for USA 94. Back then, the team took first spot in the Asian qualifying group to win the right to represent the continent at the 1994 World Cup Finals, and once there, the youngster looked their best player. Indeed, it was an al-Jaber goal that set Saudi Arabia on their way to a 2–1 victory over Morocco at USA 94.

This time around, a series of consistent performances have helped guide the Saudis to France. The hat-trick against Taiwan that put his country to the top of their group in the first round of qualifying proved al-Jaber's value as a goalscorer. But he is also the live wire in a lot of the team's approach work and has already shown that he has the confidence at the highest level to take defenders on with the ball.

Still only 26, al-Jaber has already won the Asian Cup and the Gulf Cup and has become one of the more experienced internationals in the squad. At club level, too, al-Jaber has already made it to the top. He became a national champion in 1996 when the Al-Hilal club defeated the Al-Ittihad club 1–0 in the play-off semi-final, and two goals gave his team a 2–1 victory over Al-Ahli in the final. Al-Jaber capped that success by being voted Man of the Match in Al-Hilal's Asian Cup Winners' Cup triumph when his opening goal inspired the team to a 3–1 final victory over Nagoya Grampus Eight of Japan. He then received the same award in his side's victory in the Asian Super Cup last year.

The Saudis' first attempt to qualify for the World Cup was only made as late as 1978, but their football team has come a long way since then, in fact to the point where they are now recognized as a predominant force within the Asian game. And Sami al-Jaber is their star player.

FULL NAME:	Sami al-Jaber
BORN:	11.12.72
BIRTHPLACE:	Riyadh
HEIGHT:	1.86m/6ft 1in
WEIGHT:	78kg/12st 4lbs
CLUBS:	Al Hilal
DEBUT:	1994
INTERNATIONAL HONOURS:	Asian Cup winner 1996

> ❝ **Sami al-Jaber has attracted much interest from several foreign clubs.** ❞
> — *Saudi football press*

DID YOU KNOW?
The Saudi Arabian Football Federation does not allow players to leave their home league.

THIS PAGE: AL-JABER — A HERO OF SAUDI ARABIA'S USA 94 CAMPAIGN.

OPPOSITE PAGE: SAUDI ARABIA'S MOST FAMOUS PLAYER WILL BE MAKING HIS SECOND WORLD CUP APPEARANCE IN FRANCE.

Nigeria
AMOKACHI

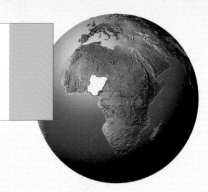

When the 1994 African Player of the Year signed for Everton that same summer, many thought that such a forceful front-runner would get a lot of opportunity to exercise his hard, accurate shooting in the still fast and furious England game. He had shown at USA 94 that he was a strong and determined player with great skills, but what was perhaps not noticed was that he was also a player who operates best when he is allowed to roam, dropping into midfield to collect the ball. This was denied him in England and his form dipped. In Turkey, he is being allowed that luxury again and his football is back to the level it was at four years ago.

His rise from obscurity to international acclaim took four years. He was first noticed at the 1990 African Nations Cup held in Algeria, where he became the youngest ever player to appear in a finals match at the age of 17. He promptly began his European career in Belgium that same year, signing for FC Bruges. After four good years there, he made what would turn out to be a mistake. He moved to Liverpool to play for Everton under Mike Walker. He never held down a regular team place in the two years he was at Goodison Park, and things got even worse after Joe Royle took over as manager. The problem was that Everton's system required him to play as a traditional centre-forward, a position he didn't know. Although he won the FA Cup, his days on Merseyside put the brakes on a very promising career.

His decision to move to Turkey was affected by his international teammate Jay Jay Okocha (see page 151), who was enjoying his football across the Bosphoros with Fenerbahçe. So, at the age of 23, the Everton reserve moved to join him in Istanbul. Besiktas' adventurous style seems more in tune with his own way of playing, and he may stay there for the rest of his career. He is another veteran of the last campaign whose form could surprise a few people who only know him from his days in England.

FULL NAME:
Daniel Amokachi
BORN:
30.12.72
BIRTHPLACE:
Kaduna
HEIGHT:
1.81m/5ft 11in
WEIGHT:
72kg/11st 5lbs
CLUBS:
DIC Bees, Bruges, Everton, Besiktas
DEBUT:
1990
INTERNATIONAL HONOURS:
African Nations Cup winner 1994

> **I am not a striker. I want to make chances for my teammates.**
> — Daniel Amokachi

DID YOU KNOW?
Fijian coach Billy Sing nominated him as FIFA Player of the Year in 1995.

THIS PAGE: DANIEL AMOKACHI — THE VETERAN IS STILL AN IMPORTANT PART OF NIGERIA'S WORLD CUP CHALLENGE.

OPPOSITE PAGE: MOVING FORWARD FOR THE EAGLES IN THE QUALIFYING MATCH AGAINST KENYA IN JANUARY 1997.

ATTACK
Colombia
ASPRILLA

FULL NAME:
Faustino Asprilla

BORN:
10.11.69

BIRTHPLACE:
Tulua

HEIGHT:
1.79m/5ft 10in

WEIGHT:
71kg/11st 3lbs

CLUBS:
Cucuta Deportivo,
Nacional de Medellin, Parma,
Newcastle United

DEBUT:
1992

To look at him when he's not right in thick of the action, you might think that Faustino Asprilla was suffering from a bad back. He lollops around with his hands on his hips, and each step seems to be costing him energy that he hasn't got. But appearances can deceive, and Asprilla is no luxury player; he works hard. Give him a sniff of the ball and immediately he springs to life. His legs seem to take on the consistency of rubber, which lets him go past defenders like they weren't there. It also allows him to control wayward passes and to take the ball away from opponents in places he shouldn't be able to reach.

The way he kicks the ball is hardly orthodox either. He taps and flicks it around with his toes, but hear former Newcastle United coach Kevin Keegan speak on the subject of the 'black gazelle' and you'll only hear praise for the man he signed from Parma for £7.5m.

Asprilla had won the Colombian Championship with Nacional before deciding to further his career in Europe. At Parma, he helped his team to the Italian Cup, the UEFA Cup and the European Cup Winners' Cup. So, when Kevin Keegan saw the opportunity to sign this supremely skilful striker, he didn't hesitate.

And yet, in his time in the Northeast of England, Asprilla has always found it difficult to hold down a regular place in the Newcastle first team. With so much competition for the right to join Alan Shearer (see page 78) in the attack, Asprilla's contribution to his club's bids for glory has been limited and sporadic. But four goals in two games at the start of last season demonstrated exactly how much talent Newcastle had on the bench. He then confirmed his form with a brilliant hat-trick for them in the European Champions League. He is considered good enough in Colombia to play on his own up front, and collected another hat-trick against Chile from that position during the course of his country's qualification programme for France 98.

❝ He's a real Newcastle player. He's quick, works hard and has flair. ❞
— *former club coach Kevin Keegan*

DID YOU KNOW?
'Asprilla' translates as aspirin. But for defenders, he causes more headaches than he cures.

THIS PAGE: FAUSTINO ASPRILLA — UNDOUBTEDLY WORLD CLASS, THE COLOMBIAN WILL RELISH THE PROSPECT OF FACING ENGLISH DEFENDERS IN THE FIRST ROUND.

OPPOSITE PAGE: ASPRILLA'S ABILITY TO HANG IN THE AIR IS ONE OF HIS GREATEST STRENGTHS.

Morocco
BASSIR

There seems to be a Maradona of just about every geographical region of the world these days, and in the Spanish region of Galicia it's Saleheddine Bassir. He plays his club football at Deportivo de la Coruña, having arrived in the summer of 1996 to join up with teammate Noureddine Naybet (see page 202). In lighting up the team he has now gained the nickname 'Maradona of the Desert'. And in his case, it is easy to understand how the comparison has been made. Bassir's physical stature and the position he plays certainly remind you of the Argentinian. Nominally a centre-forward, Bassir will frequently drop back into midfield to pick up the ball, and his speed, skill and creative play are some of the more salient features of Morocco's footballing style.

In midfield, Bassir is always looking to get involved, and many of his team's better moves pass through him. In attack, he shows good positional sense and is a tremendous opportunist striker. He has a powerful and accurate shot and can create goalscoring positions from the slightest of half-chances. He is also often to be seen playing out towards the flanks, where he takes on the mantle of a remarkably fast, hungry winger who likes to take the ball to defenders from the right side of the attack. From this position, his pace can take him past full-backs into dangerous positions where he can cross for a teammate or cut inside and go for goal himself.

And it is as a goalscorer that Bassir is most useful to this increasingly impressive Moroccan side. He netted four times in six games as Morocco swept aside the much-fancied Ghanaian team in qualifying. Goals from him have also recently given the Moroccans an eye-opening 2–0 win over Olympic Champions Nigeria and a creditable 2–2 draw with Croatia. Although he did not appear at USA 94, Bassir has now picked up over 30 caps for his country and is their major source of goals. Many eyes are on the Nigerians this summer, but watch out for Saleheddine Bassir's Morocco. They could be the surprise of the tournament.

FULL NAME:	Saleheddine Bassir
BORN:	12.9.72
BIRTHPLACE:	Casablanca
HEIGHT:	1.68m/5ft 6in
WEIGHT:	64kg/10st 1lb
CLUBS:	Raja Casablanca, Al Hilal, Deportivo de la Coruña

66 Bassir is always looking to get involved, and many of his team's better moves pass through him. **99**

DID YOU KNOW?
Bassir scored the goal in Sierra Leone way back in April 1997 that ensured Morocco's fourth World Cup qualification.

THIS PAGE: SALAHEDDINE BASSIR — MOROCCO'S GOALSCORING HERO IN QUALIFYING.

OPPOSITE PAGE: THE MOROCCANS ARE MOST PEOPLE'S FAVOURITES FOR AN EARLY EXIT, BUT BASSIR WILL BE A CONSTANT DANGER TO DEFENDERS.

Argentina
BATISTUTA

FULL NAME:
Gabriel Omar Batistuta

BORN:
1.2.69

BIRTHPLACE:
Reconquista, Santa Fe

HEIGHT:
1.89m/6ft 2in

WEIGHT:
80kg/12st 8lbs

CLUBS:
Newell's Old Boys, River Plate,
Boca Juniors, Fiorentina

DEBUT:
1989

INTERNATIONAL HONOURS:
Copa America winner 1991

❝ **Batistuta is one of the best strikers in the world. He's fearless, powerful and a real team leader.** ❞
— *club teammate and Uruguayan international Paolo Montero*

DID YOU KNOW?
Batistuta has scored in a record 11 consecutive Serie A games.

THIS PAGE: GABRIEL BATISTUTA —
FIORENTINA FANS WILL TELL YOU HE'S
THE BEST GOALSCORER IN THE WORLD.

OPPOSITE PAGE: 'BATIGOL' CELEBRATES
ANOTHER STRIKE AGAINST BULGARIA
AT USA 94.

Argentina's all-time top scorer has been likened to Mario Kempes (see page 10), the striker who led Argentina to World Cup glory in 1978. Physically, the similarities are there. Both are strong, powerful players. Both are good in the air and on the ground, and both have worn their hair long. But 'Batigol' is even more of an out-and-out striker than his predecessor who rarely got involved in anything outside the opposition's penalty area. When he has a barren spell, Batigol is accused of not contributing to the team effort. But his critics – none from Florence – are always silenced when he suddenly appears from nowhere to bury the ball in the back of the net. His goals have lifted *La Viola* from the obscurity of Serie B to the spotlight of Italian football. He is the captain, the idol of the fans and very much the leader of the team.

Batistuta made an unglamorous start in professional football in September 1988 when he appeared for Newell's Old Boys in a 1–0 away defeat by San Martin in the isolated northern town of Tucuman. He went on to play for three clubs in Argentina, spending one season at each and scoring a respectable, but hardly earth-shattering, total of 24 goals in 75 first-team appearances. It was not until he was playing for Boca Juniors that a video of him in action was seen in Florence. He had previously appeared in the Viareggio tournament in Italy in 1989, scoring a hat-trick, but this had gone unnoticed and he moved to Fiorentina without great ceremony.

Having been shunned for ten months by Argentine national coach Daniel Passarella (see page 168), the man who got four goals at USA 94, he was called back to the team on Halloween 1997, after Argentina had secured their place in France. Although his country qualified without him, Italians recognize that he has consistently been his club's best player since signing in 1991. And they know that his return to the Argentine national team will undoubtedly boost his country's chances of challenging for their third World Cup victory.

ATTACK
Holland
BERGKAMP

One player above all others who can lift the Dutch to their third World Cup final place is Arsenal's Dennis Bergkamp. He made his international debut just after Italy 90 and has been a key part of Holland's last two campaigns. His goals at home and away against England secured qualification for USA 94, and he scored two more at the Finals. He scored a hat-trick against Wales in qualification for France 98, and the goal that clinched a World Cup place for the Dutch this time was his 33rd for Holland, putting him two short of the all-time record.

The youngster named after Scotland legend Denis Law joined Ajax when he was only 12. Such was his natural talent that he was picked by technical director Johan Cruyff (see page 95) to play his league debut for Ajax as early as 1986, while he was still 16. He was part of the victorious European Cup Winners' Cup team of that season and became joint top scorer in the Dutch League in 1991 with PSV's Romario (see page 68). There was no competition for him after Romario went to Barcelona, and he was the league's outright top scorer and Player of the Year for the following two seasons.

In total, he netted 103 times in 185 games for Ajax, and although he only got in 11 goals in 52 Serie A games at Inter Milan, he did manage the same number in 11 UEFA Cup games as Inter won the trophy, his second medal in that competition. He was injured in his second season there and Arsenal bought him at a discount price of £7.5m in 1996. Injuries again kept him in and out of the team in his first season at Highbury, and a spate of yellow cards earned him a suspension at the beginning of the 97/98 season. But when he has been available for selection, he has been the best player in the Premiership. He is not the fastest. He doesn't have to be. 'It is not speed that gives you the option to do things, it is balance', he says. The Dutch are hoping he steers clear of injury before he drives down to France.

FULL NAME:
Dennis Bergkamp
BORN:
10.5.69
BIRTHPLACE:
Amsterdam
HEIGHT:
1.85m/6ft 1in
WEIGHT:
78kg/12st 4lbs
CLUBS:
Ajax, Inter Milan, Arsenal
DEBUT:
1990

66 The most talented player in England. 99
— *former Liverpool player and Scotland international Alan Hansen*

DID YOU KNOW?
He once scored in a record ten successive games in the Dutch League.

THIS PAGE: DENNIS BERGKAMP — QUITE POSSIBLY THE GREATEST PLAYER IN THE WORLD AT THE MOMENT.

OPPOSITE PAGE: THE MASTER AT WORK AGAINST BELGIUM IN QUALIFYING 3–1 ON SEPTEMBER 6TH, 1997.

ATTACK
Spain
'RAUL' BLANCO

He's been in the team for less than two years but this inventive striker already looks like being a permanent fixture in the Spanish side for at least another decade. He scores a lot of goals from his advanced midfielder/attacker position through supporting the attack from the right, and he sets up a lot more.

Raul was born in Madrid and has declared himself 'a Madrid boy', uninterested in ever moving to Barcelona or Milan. Argentinian national coach Jorge Valdano was the man who gave him his chance in the Real Madrid first team and he points to the player's immense determination as the key to his success – that and some wonderful skills and the goalscoring abilities that are always at a premium in the Spanish league. In the 1994/95 season, as a 17-year-old debutant, Raul immediately made his name at the Bernabeu, scoring in his second game. The hat-trick he scored in the 6–1 thrashing of Ferencvaros from Hungary the following season was the point where it was fully realized just how crucial to the Madrid team he had become. Even with players around with so much more experience, he is the one who plays well even when his teammates don't.

Though he was immediately catapulted to fame, Raul is a staunch advocate of the perceived need in Spain to produce more home-grown talent. 'Every player has to start somewhere,' he has said. 'If the clubs didn't worry about youth teams, where would they get their players?' The answer is that the clubs would import players, but in Spain, that is not thought to help the prospects of the national team.

'I want to win the World Cup with Spain,' says their most brilliant prospect. His country surely has the best chance they've had since they hosted the Finals in 1982, and their supporters will travel over the Pyrenees in force in the hope of celebrating Raul's 21st birthday with a World Cup win. The rest of the world might think them over-confident, but the difference this player makes could be the push the Spanish need to justify their FIFA ranking.

FULL NAME:
Raul Gonzalez Blanco

BORN:
27.6.77

BIRTHPLACE:
Madrid

HEIGHT:
1.80m/5ft 11in

WEIGHT:
69kg/10st 12lbs

CLUBS:
Real Madrid

DEBUT:
1996

> 66 **Raul is destined to make his mark on a whole generation, and not just in Spanish football.** 99
> — *coach Javier Clemente*

DID YOU KNOW?
Raul was Real Madrid's youngest ever first-team debutant, aged 17 years and four months.

THIS PAGE: RAUL GONZALEZ BLANCO — TEENAGE SENSATION WHO MANY THINK COULD BECOME SPAIN'S GREATEST EVER PLAYER.

OPPOSITE PAGE: IN ACTION FOR REAL, THE ONLY TEAMS RAUL HAS EVER WANTED TO PLAY FOR.

ATTACK
Italy
CASIRAGHI

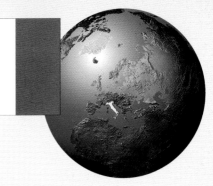

The man who scored the goal that beat Russia and qualified Italy for the World Cup is now in line to reclaim his place as a first-choice starter for his national team, while the Russians must be sick of the sight of him. Casiraghi had previously scored both goals in a 2–1 victory when the teams met at Euro 96, when the Lazio striker was a surprise replacement for Juve's Fabrizio Ravanelli (see page 66). The first goal that day came as a result of a poor clearance from the Russian goalkeeper Cherchesov, and Casiraghi was clinical in dispatching Angelo Di Livio's pass. The winner came just after half time as Gianfranco Zola (see page 93) played a perfect ball into feet that 'Gigi' took in his stride and buried in the back of the net. Had his first-half back-heel flick gone just the other side of the post, comparisons with Paolo Rossi's performances that helped Italy to World Cup glory in 1982 would have been hard to ignore.

Like many strikers who play in Italy's notoriously low-scoring Serie A, Casiraghi's goalscoring record makes him look an inconsistent striker. But goals will always eventually come to capable players who are as concentrated as Casiraghi. Having shown a modest return of 28 League goals in four seasons, as Monza floated between Serie B and Serie C, Casiraghi signed for Juventus in 1991/92, where he immediately won a place in the first team. But he was never prolific there either, and it wasn't until after he transferred to Lazio in 1993 that he started to look like a true international class striker.

But Casiraghi has never been an out-and-out goalscorer. He is a player who is always looking for the ball in the build up, and some of his approach work is quite superb. Nevertheless, he is not a midfielder, and Italy's enormous wealth of talent in attack means that Casiraghi will have to wait with Ravanelli, Zola and Vialli (see page 86), not to mention Filippo Inzaghi, Enrico Chiesa, Alessandro Del Piero, Christian Vieri and Roberto Baggio, to see who coach Cesare Maldini selects.

FULL NAME:
Pierluigi Casiraghi

BORN:
4.3.69

BIRTHPLACE:
Monza

HEIGHT:
1.82m/6ft

WEIGHT:
78kg/12st 4lbs

CLUBS:
Monza, Juventus, Lazio

DEBUT:
1991

> **66** The first game is always very difficult, but to come here and score two goals in such a stadium is great. **99**
> — *Pierluigi Casiraghi after his goals defeated Russia at Wembley in 1996*

DID YOU KNOW?
Casiraghi missed a last-minute sitter against the Czech Republic just three days after his goals had defeated Russia at Euro 96. Italy lost 2–1.

THIS PAGE: PIERLUIGI CASIRAGHI — A LETHAL SHOT HAS MADE HIM ONE OF ITALY'S MOST FEARED STRIKERS.

OPPOSITE PAGE: CASIRAGHI ENDED QUALIFYING JUST AHEAD OF THE COMPETITION FOR A PLACE IN ITALY'S STARTING LINE-UP.

Argentina
CRESPO

FULL NAME:
Hernan Jorge Crespo

BORN:
5.7.75

BIRTHPLACE:
Florida, Buenos Aires

HEIGHT:
1.80m/5ft 11in

WEIGHT:
78kg/12st 4lbs

CLUBS:
River Plate, Fiorentina, Parma

DEBUT:
1995

C hallenging for a place in Argentina's starting line up is a young opportunist striker who has been appearing at the far post for club and country on an increasingly regular basis over the last few years. It is a shame for Hernan Crespo that his teammate Daniel Ortega (see page 153) has been pushed up front to play alongside the recently recalled Gabriel Batistuta (see page 22). That is just the position where Crespo operates best. With Fiorentina's famous marksman operating slightly to the right, the lesser known Crespo has been able to find space on the left. His reading of the final ball is so good that he often gets himself into positions in the six-yard box where a simple tap in is all he needs to add to his goalscoring tally.

He started playing for River Plate at the end of 1993. By the end of the season, his 13 goals had earned him the regular first-team place he was to keep throughout his three years at the club. In 1996 he transferred to Italy, and that move has put him even more in the spotlight in his home country. Italian football is widely followed in Argentina, and while he has yet to become a sure starter for his country, his performances for Parma have helped his international career along. Batistuta is likely to be Argentina's greatest hope of goals, but if the Fiorentina captain is absent for any reason, or off form, Crespo will undoubtedly be the man sent in to replace him.

It is still possible that Crespo will start, however, even if Ortega partners Batistuta up front. Crespo is becoming much more than just a goalscorer. He can drop into midfield where he shows a surety of touch in Argentina's patient build-ups. If the 1986 World Cup winners ever find they have to chase the game, any combination of Batigol, Crespo and Ortega playing up front, will provide one of the greatest challenges any defence will have to deal with in France.

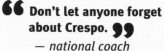

" Don't let anyone forget about Crespo. "
— *national coach*
Daniel Passarella

DID YOU KNOW?
Crespo scored 24 goals in 62 appearances for River Plate.

THIS PAGE: HERNAN CRESPO — CELEBRATING ANOTHER GOAL FOR PARMA.

OPPOSITE PAGE: CRESPO WILL BE HOPING HE IS SELECTED TO PLAY ALONGSIDE BATISTUTA IN FRANCE.

ATTACK
Iran
DAEI

A li Daei has come to the World Cup the hard way. His home near the Caspian Sea, in the northwest of the country, near the border with the former Soviet Republic of Azerbaijan, is notorious for its extremely cold winters, and 'Shahriar' (the King) is the first person ever from Ardabil to play for the national team. Daei and his five brothers could only play for their local team in the summer months and their father was discouraging of their pastime. 'My father was against my playing football during the school year,' Daei recalls. 'I remember I used to leave home without my football kit and my mother would smuggle it out for me so that I could play.'

But Daei soon became a regular on the Ardabil All-Star team and played friendly matches against out-of-town teams. Then in 1988 he went to Tehran's University of Industrial Studies to study metallurgy and started scoring regularly for Second Division Taxirani. He went on to become the First Division's top scorer three years in a row with Tejarat, scoring a record 27 goals in 30 league games in 1992. In 1993 he was called up to the national team, coming on as a substitute for Samad Marfavi for the last 20 minutes of the 1994 World Cup qualifier against Oman. Daei didn't score and the game ended in a disappointing 0–0 draw, but the new striker hit the crossbar twice and consolidated his place in the team. He fell out with coach Mohammed Mayeli Kohan while he was playing for al-Saad in Qatar and was dropped from the team, but now those differences have been patched up and Daei is back in the fold.

He has already shown he is capable of making the grade in the Bundesliga and was top scorer in the Asian Cup in 1996. He managed an astonishing 22 international goals that year, and his partnership with Asian Player of the Year Khodadad Azizi is one of the most feared strike forces in Asia.

FULL NAME:
Ali Daei

BORN:
21.1.69

BIRTHPLACE:
Ardabil

HEIGHT:
1.89m/6ft 2in

WEIGHT:
82kg/12st 13lbs

CLUBS:
Javanan Ardabil,
Esteghlal Ardabil, Taxirani Tehran,
Tejarat Tehran,
Persepolis International
(now Pirouzi), al-Saad,
Arminia Bielefeld

DEBUT:
1993

66 **My real dream is to reach the 1998 World Cup finals with Iran.** 99
— Ali Daei after the Asian Cup

DID YOU KNOW?
Daei's first club was a family affair. Almost the entire squad was made up of his brothers, cousins and uncles.

THIS PAGE: ALI DAEI — THE IRANIAN STAR IS FROM UNLIKELY FOOTBALLING STOCK.

OPPOSITE PAGE: DAEI WAS DROPPED FROM THE TEAM AFTER CRITICIZING THE TEAM COACH WITHIN EARSHOT.

ATTACK
France
DUGARRY

Barcelona felt they needed two players to replace the departing Ronaldo, so they signed Dugarry as well as the Brazilian sensation Rivaldo from Deportivo. It is the latter who is expected to be a more integral part of the Catalan club, but this attacking workhorse remains the host nation's best hope of goals in France 98. He is their most consistent front-runner.

Has never had a spectacular goalscoring record but has a habit of making vital strikes like the two he scored for Bordeaux when they beat Milan in the 1996 UEFA Cup. It was this performance that prompted the Italian giants to sign him. However, his time there was an unhappy one and he left after one season. During this time he played only ten games, scoring a respectable four goals in the defensively tight Serie A. The reason for the low appearance count was that arriving with a serious injury, he missed the crucial start to the season and took a long time to get into contention for the regular first-team place he was never to win.

His international form suffered as a result, to the extent that he was prompted to say: 'I'm playing badly here [for France] because they won't let me play there.' He left Milan for Barcelona in the summer of 1996, claiming that his former teammates were more interested in playing for themselves than they were in playing for the team.

Despite this setback to his career, however, he stayed in the international reckoning and was highly impressive in Le Tournoi 97. He dominated even the normally aerially strong English defence; Gary Neville is not the tallest of defenders but it is rare for Gary Pallister to be found wanting in that department. Dugarry remains France's best hope of goals and will also be used as a target man to bring the highly talented French midfield up into goalscoring positions.

FULL NAME:
Christophe Dugarry

BORN:
24.3.72

BIRTHPLACE
Bordeaux

HEIGHT:
1.88m/6ft 2in

WEIGHT:
82kg/12st 13lbs

CLUBS:
Bordeaux, AC Milan, Barcelona

DEBUT:
1995

❝ We could have signed him but we didn't want to. ❞
— *Jesus Gil y Gil, the loquacious president of Atletico Madrid*

DID YOU KNOW?
Against Romania at Euro 96, Dugarry scored what was easily the silliest goal of the Finals.

THIS PAGE: CHRISTOPHE DUGARRY — NO OTHER ATTACKER IN THE FRENCH SET-UP HAS PROVEN HIMSELF AT INTERNATIONAL LEVEL.

OPPOSITE PAGE: SKIPPING PAST THE OPPOSITION IN FRANCE'S 2–2 DRAW AGAINST ITALY IN THE 1997 TOURNOI DE FRANCE.

Scotland
GALLACHER

Blackburn Rovers' attacker has been a sensation at both club and international level in 1997. In a career spanning a decade, his goalscoring record has always been respectable for a journeyman striker, but not the stuff of international glory. However, the man who had hitherto failed to gain a regular place in the national team began this season with a goal blitz for both club and country.

He scored both goals when Scotland defeated group winners Austria 2–0 at Hampden Park. He scored two more in the 4–1 defeat of Belarus last September, getting onto the end of a free-kick after only six minutes and then coolly rounding the keeper for his second. It was Gallacher again who recovered from an Achilles tendon injury to open the scoring with a firm header in the defeat of Latvia that saw the Scots qualify for France 98. Later in that same game, his chip cleared the goalkeeper's head only to hit the crossbar. Fortunately for Scotland, Gordon Durie was on hand to score their second goal. After that, the Latvians never looked like pulling off a shock result. Scotland only had to wait a matter of hours to hear that Spain had won their final match against the Faroe Islands and that the Scots had qualified. 'We did a very professional job,' said coach Craig Brown as he left for France to sort out his team's hotel accommodation for the tournament. The basis of that job was Gallacher's opening goal and his contribution to the second.

Gallacher is an indefatigable front runner who is always jockeying for position. With the surprise retirement from international football of Duncan Ferguson, Gallacher's current rich vein of form makes him the ideal replacement for the Everton hitman. He may not have Ferguson's height and weight, and he may not be able to hang in the air like his predecessor, but with the ball on the ground, he is as quick as lightning over a couple of metres. He has also now reached such a level of confidence that whenever he finds himself within shooting range, he no longer ever seems to consider that he might not score.

FULL NAME:
Kevin Gallacher
BORN:
23.11.66
BIRTHPLACE:
Clydebank
HEIGHT:
1.75m/5ft 9in
WEIGHT:
72kg/11st 5lbs
CLUBS:
Dundee United, Coventry City, Blackburn Rovers
DEBUT:
1988

66 Kevin Gallacher's on fire. **99**
— *national coach Craig Brown*

DID YOU KNOW?
In total, Gallacher scored six times in four games back in the Scotland team.

THIS PAGE: KEVIN GALLACHER — SCOTLAND WILL NEED THEIR NEW GOALSCORING SENSATION TO KEEP UP HIS FORM IN FRONT OF GOAL.

OPPOSITE PAGE: CHALLENGING THE ESTONIAN DEFENCE IN ONE OF THE FEW GAMES HE HASN'T SCORED IN RECENTLY.

Austria
HERZOG

Austria are an improving team and this vastly experienced Werder Bremen playmaker is a regular on the score sheet for both club and country. He is the source of much of his club's attacking flair, and when he missed the early part of this season after going under the surgeon's knife for a recurrent toe injury, the Bundesliga side struggled in his absence. Now fully restored to fitness, Herzog has rediscovered the form he lost during a season with Bayern Munich two years ago, and has built on a fine 1996/97 that saw him rattle in 15 League goals.

A member of the Austrian side that went home humiliated after the first round of Italia 90, Andy Herzog is one of coach Herbert Prohaska's old guard. For this campaign, however, the Austrians have a lot of promising new talent and Herzog will be driven by the knowledge that he is probably getting his last crack at football's biggest prize.

One example of the way Austrian football has improved recently was the vitally important 1–0 home victory over USA 94 semi-finalists Sweden in qualifying. The Swedes still have a very strong side, but were unlucky to find themselves in a highly competitive group that also happened to include Europe's most improved team. They were unlucky to come up against Andy Herzog too. He scored the winner on the big occasion and the Austrians began to sense that they could qualify for France. Before the return leg, Herzog tried to lower the ever-increasing expectations of the Austrian public by saying that he was 'afraid it was quite possible that we only get a draw in Sweden and that the Scots, with a superior goal difference, could go to France as group winners'. In the event, Herzog scored the winner again in another 1–0 win and the Austrians went to the top of the table.

Herzog is a player who seems to relish the big occasion. He will also be hoping to wipe away the memories of that poor showing in Italy by lighting up France 98 with his exquisite passing and trademark bursts into the box.

FULL NAME:	Andreas Herzog
BORN:	10.9.68
BIRTHPLACE:	Vienna
HEIGHT:	1.83m/6ft
WEIGHT:	80kg/12st 8lbs
CLUBS:	Admiral Wacker, Rapid Vienna, Vienna, Bayern Munich, Werder Bremen
DEBUT:	1988

66 That's absolute nonsense. **99**
— *Andreas Herzog on suggestions that he might miss the World Cup through injury*

DID YOU KNOW?
Herzog was told he would never play for Austria again after missing a friendly against Russia in 1994. He was reprieved seven months later.

THIS PAGE: ANDREAS HERZOG — A REGULAR STARTER IN EUROPE'S MOST IMPROVED TEAM.

OPPOSITE PAGE: HERZOG WILL BE NOW BE MORE OPTIMISTIC THAT HIS TEAM CAN BE ONE OF THE SURPRISES OF THE TOURNAMENT.

Nigeria
KANU

FULL NAME:
Nwankwo Kanu

BORN:
1.8.76

BIRTHPLACE:
Owerri

HEIGHT:
1.97m/6ft 6in

WEIGHT:
80kg/12st 8lbs

CLUBS:
Federal Works,
Iwuanyanwu Nationale,
Ajax, Inter Milan

The blossoming career of the 1996 African Player of the Year was very nearly ended when Inter Milan's doctors noticed that he had a congenital heart defect. Bruno Caru, Inter's cardiologist, believed their new signing would never again be able to cope with the stresses of professional football, but Kanu has successfully overcome reparative surgery to return as the spearhead of the Nigerian strike force. He is not the most prolific goalscorer, averaging rather less than a goal every two games over his club career, but he is a quick and clever attacker whose presence in the Inter Milan team was sorely missed while he was in hospital in America.

Kanu first signed a professional contract in 1992 after being spotted playing for a local amateur side. In his one season at Nationale, he won a Championship medal and was selected by Fanny Amun, the coach of the national under-17s, to play in the World Championships in Japan. His five goals lifted the Golden Eaglets to victory and gave him the opportunity of a move to Ajax in the summer of 1993. In Holland, he won three consecutive Championships, collecting the domestic Double twice, but it was a year before he scored for the first team. His early failure to make his mark at the Ajax's made him a surprise omission from Nigeria's African Nations Cup winning squad of 1994 and also from the World Cup squad. But his part in the Amsterdam club's UEFA Champions League victory in 1995 persuaded Inter Milan to sign him for a bargain £2m that summer.

This move and four goals at the Olympics, where he captained the victorious team, lifted his career to new heights, but it was then that the faulty aortic valve was noticed. Inter Milan and Ajax have been at loggerheads over the affair, but Kanu is getting on with his football again. If he can repeat feats like his last-minute equalizer against a virtually full-strength Brazilian side in the Olympic semi-final and the cool finishing of his extra-time goal that took Nigeria to the final, the Eagles may improve on their second-round place at USA 94.

> **Giving up football is just unthinkable. I will fight to the very end.**
> — *Nwankwo Kanu just before his heart surgery*

DID YOU KNOW?
Kanu scored 25 goals in 54 League games in his three years at Ajax.

THIS PAGE: NWANKWO KANU — BEAT THE ODDS TO RETURN TO FIRST-CLASS FOOTBALL.

OPPOSITE PAGE: KANU IS HELD ALOFT BY HIS TEAMMATES AFTER THE DEFEAT OF ARGENTINA IN THE 1996 OLYMPIC GAMES.

Germany
KLINSMANN

FULL NAME:
Jürgen Klinsmann

BORN:
30.7.64

BIRTHPLACE:
Goppingen

HEIGHT:
1.83m/6ft

WEIGHT:
76kg/12st

CLUBS:
Stuttgart Kickers, VfB Stuttgart,
Inter Milan, Monaco,
Tottenham Hotspur,
Bayern Munich, Sampdoria

DEBUT:
1987

INTERNATIONAL HONOURS:
World Cup winner 1990, European
Championship winner 1996

❝ I don't fit in. ❞
*— Klinsmann to Franz
Beckenbauer (see page 169)*

DID YOU KNOW?
Klinsmann will win his 100th
international cap in France.

THIS PAGE: JÜRGEN KLINSMANN –
TIGHTENING HIS BOOTLACES FOR A LAST
WORLD CUP.

OPPOSITE PAGE: MAINTAINING HIS BALANCE
UNDER PRESSURE. HE'S OUTSIDE THE
PENALTY AREA HERE.

The career of this undoubtedly world-class striker has taken him half way around Western Europe. Until now at least, he has never settled down in one place for long. But throughout the turmoil he has proved himself at the highest level. In winning the UEFA Cup with Bayern Munich, he scored 15 goals, an all-time record in European club competition. France 98 will be his last chance to complete a hat-trick of titles with Germany.

Klinsmann joined Stuttgart Kickers at 17. Within three years he was playing in the top flight of the Bundesliga for Stuttgart's most illustrious team, VfB. Like England's Paul Ince (see page 132), he had a tough time at Inter Milan, but that spell aside, and despite a few differences with various colleagues down the years, his performances on the pitch have never left anyone in doubt of his extraordinary ability.

He has been an international since 1987 and played a major part in West Germany's success in 1990, as well as helping his newly united country to the quarter-finals of USA 94. He was promoted to the national captaincy after the retirement of Lothar Matthäus. His differences with the former West German sweeper were clear, as were those with Spurs supremo Alan Sugar. He has made a few enemies on the pitch too with his habit of losing his footing in the penalty area, but his skills have only improved with age. He is nowadays just as likely to dance past his marker and score a goal as he is to fling himself to the ground.

He has always expressed a love for Italy but threatened to quit football altogether when he left Inter, saying he wanted to return home to Germany to complete his university studies. He went to the relative quiet of Monaco instead, spent one year in London, decided he couldn't live in Germany and now claims he is happy to be back in Italy. He says that he enjoys the lifestyle there and that he plans to stay in the country after his imminent retirement. He'll want to win the World Cup again first.

Holland
KLUIVERT

AC Milan and Holland's latest goalscoring sensation has had some fast growing up to do. As a teenage star in the all-conquering Ajax, he was convicted of manslaughter after his reckless driving caused the death of a theatre director. For that, he was given a two-year suspended sentence and ordered to do 240 hours community service. He has since had rape charges brought against himself and three friends by a 20-year-old Dutch woman. These were dropped after Kluivert admitted having sex with the girl but denied rape. Having transformed from hero to villain in his own country before his 21st birthday, he now recognizes that he has to prove himself both on and off the pitch.

Kluivert is the most talented striker to come out of the Ajax system since Dennis Bergkamp (see page 25), and he started showing his knack for scoring vital goals early in his career. In his debut season in the first team, the 18-year-old scored the winner for Ajax in the European Cup Final against AC Milan. He then managed the winner in the 1–0 European Super Cup victory. The following summer, and a fortnight before his 20th birthday, he scrambled in a late effort against hosts England in the 1996 European Championships. It was only a consolation goal in terms of the outcome of the match, his side lost 4–1, but in the event, it was enough to see Holland scrape through to the second round on goal difference at the expense of Scotland.

He was plagued by a knee injury throughout Euro 96 and fans didn't see much of him, but it is testament to his perceived value to the team that the youngster was still selected by his country for a major international competition when he was clearly not fully fit. He's not the fastest but he is good in the air, where he can hang for ages before delivering a header as strong as a shot. He will let his football do the talking in France.

FULL NAME:
Patrick Kluivert
BORN:
1.7.76
BIRTHPLACE:
Amsterdam
HEIGHT:
1.90m/6ft 3in
WEIGHT:
77kg/12st 2lbs
CLUBS:
Ajax, AC Milan
DEBUT:
1996

> **I shall have to win the supporters' respect back again.**
> — *Patrick Kluivert*

DID YOU KNOW?
Kluivert played in the Ajax youth system from the age of seven.

THIS PAGE: PATRICK KLUIVERT — THE BOY WITH A LOT TO PROVE WILL HOPE TO BE CELEBRATING A LOT MORE GOALS THIS SUMMER.

OPPOSITE PAGE: HOLLAND'S CENTRE FORWARD ABOUT TO ATTACK THE BELGIAN DEFENCE IN QUALIFYING 3–1 IN ROTTERDAM.

Denmark
B LAUDRUP

66 **I realized that if the move to Rangers did not come off, it would have been very difficult for my career. But it is the best move I have ever made.** 99
— *Brian Laudrup*

DID YOU KNOW?
Brian and his brother are the sons of former Danish international, confusingly named Finn Laudrup.

THIS PAGE: BRIAN LAUDRUP — THE YOUNGER BROTHER IN DENMARK'S FEARED ATTACKING PARTNERSHIP.

OPPOSITE PAGE: UNLIKE HIS BROTHER, THE RANGERS PLAYER HAS ALREADY WON INTERNATIONAL HONOURS WITH DENMARK.

This highly experienced international made his debut in Thailand in the Kings Cup in January 1988, and has since won over 80. He was made Danish player of the year in 1989 and unlike his older brother Michael (see page 49) took part in the European Championship win of 1992, where the then AC Milan star was the inspiration behind his country's historic 2–0 final victory over hot favourites Germany.

However, like his brother, he has dazzling ball skills, which – as well as being put to good effect for set pieces – can also be seen in his frequent, and often successful, attempts to dribble the ball into the net. His three goals in three games were among the only high points of Denmark's attempt to retain the European Championship in 1996.

Brian Laudrup first left Denmark for Bayer Uerdingen for £650,000, then a Danish record fee. By the time he moved to Munich, he was valued at a Bundesliga record £2m. He subsequently signed for Fiorentina for £3.5m and from there went to Scotland for £2.4m to become part of the most successful Rangers team of all time. His contribution was recognized with the 1995 Scottish Player of the Year award after his first season in that country. He won that award again in 1997, as the Glasgow club equalled city rivals Celtic's record of nine successive League Championships.

In Denmark's qualification for France, he scored over Greece and also got the late equalizer that gave the Danes a point against Croatia in Zagreb. It was from a Brian Laudrup in-swinger that striker Miklos Molnar (see page 58) delivered the final blow against Croatia in Copenhagen after Brian and his brother Michael had scored the opening two goals. That result effectively put the Danes straight through to France, while the Croatians went into the UEFA play-offs as the second-placed team.

He takes most of Denmark's corner kicks and his effectiveness in this role was recognized by Bosnian coach Fuad Muzurovic, who duly noted that 'Denmark were very dangerous after free-kicks and corners', after his team had been beaten in Copenhagen. When Bosnia surprisingly beat Denmark 3–0 in the return match, Brian Laudrup was a noticeable absentee.

Denmark
M LAUDRUP

Denmark's most experienced player made his international debut as an 18-year-old and, apart from a time when he fell out of the team under Richard Moller-Neilsen, he has been their best player for an astonishing decade and a half. Juventus won the chase to sign the highly promising teenager in 1983, but Michael Laudrup took a while to make a name for himself in Turin. In fact, he was loaned out to relegation-bound Lazio for two years before returning to help Juve win the Italian League in 1986, the year of his World Cup Finals debut.

Johan Cruyff (see page 95) noticed his skills when the Dutch legend was team coach at Barcelona, and Laudrup's time in the Catalan capital coincided with his rise to true international prominence. His value to the Barcelona side that won four successive Spanish league titles was apparently not recognized by the club, until they sold him to rivals Real Madrid. It then became quite apparent that Michael Laudrup was one of the most effective, if not the most effective, players in Spain at that time. Barcelona were suddenly no longer the best team in Spain. His new club regained the title in Michael Laudrup's first season there.

He plays his best football as an attacking midfielder. He likes to drift out wide and beat opponents with his exquisite ball control and deceptive pace, but he can also play exremely effectively as an out-and-out striker. Michael Laudrup is an accomplished goalscorer who can create and take chances out of almost nothing. However, coach Bo Johannson is likely to use his vast experience as a provider in the centre of the pitch, not least because the Danes have an embarrassment of riches up front already.

Michael Laudrup was part of the 1988 European Championship team but did not appear in the victory of 1992 after failing to resolve a dispute with the then national coach Richard Moller-Neilsen. But now that he is back as integral part of the team, and his formidable style is well known throughout the world, he will be the player teams fear most when they face the mighty Danes.

FULL NAME:
Michael Laudrup

BORN:
15.6.64

BIRTHPLACE:
Copenhagen

HEIGHT:
1.85m/6ft

WEIGHT:
80kg/12st 8lbs

CLUBS:
Brondby, FC Kobenhavn, Lazio, Juventus, Barcelona, Real Madrid, Visselkobe, Ajax

DEBUT:
1982

66 **We need you, Michael.** 99
— *Catalan TV after their idol's move to Madrid*

DID YOU KNOW?
Michael Laudrup played for Barcelona when they beat Real Madrid 5–0 in 1994 and for Real when they beat Barcelona 5–0 the following season.

THIS PAGE: MICHAEL LAUDRUP — THE ELDER OF DENMARK'S FOOTBALLING BROTHERS IS LOOKING TO ADD TO HIS EXTENSIVE TROPHY ROOM.

OPPOSITE PAGE: MICHAEL SHOWS BRAZIL'S RICARDO A THING OR TWO ABOUT BALL CONTROL.

Spain
LUIS ENRIQUE

FULL NAME:
Luis Enrique Martinez Garcia

BORN:
8.5.70

BIRTHPLACE:
Gijon

HEIGHT:
1.79m/5ft 10in

WEIGHT:
72kg/11st 5lbs

CLUBS:
SP Promesas, Deportivo La Brana, Sporting, Sporting Gijon, Real Madrid, Barcelona

DEBUT:
1991

Although he was already an experienced international, Luis Enrique spent far too long as little more than a squad player at Real Madrid following his move to the Spanish capital from his native Asturias. The boy from the north of Spain was then snatched from the Castilian club by rivals Barcelona in 1996. His contract at the Bernabeu had expired and he was immediately offered a regular place in the Catalan club's first team. His incredible stamina and consistently excellent performances there as a right-sided utility player have now also made him an automatic first choice for the national team.

He used to play further up into the midfield for his club, but although he still weighs in with a fair few goals, he is now often expected to run the flank as an attacking wing-back in the place of Albert Ferrer. Although this is not his natural position, Luis Enrique has adapted well to his new role. He is a player who is always prepared to give everything to his performance and will run hard throughout the entire game, whatever the scoreline. At club level, he has experienced several occasions where his team has been winning the game by a good half dozen goals, but Luis Enrique sees that as no reason to ease off towards the end. His total commitment to the cause means he will chase for every ball until the final whistle.

When he gets forward, he is always looking for an opportunity to get into a goalscoring position, picking out his territory in the penalty area. Luis Enrique's goals are rarely beautiful, though. He is more likely to score with an outstretched foot in a scramble in the six-yard box than at the end of one of his trademark runs down the wing. However, his importance to the team becomes apparent when he also appears in the ruck at the other end, desperately trying to get the ball away from his own goalmouth. One of coach Javier Clemente's greatest assets is this battling utility player who has also consistently been one of his more likely sources of a goal.

> **❝ I've had to adapt to various positions but I still consider myself a forward. ❞**
> — *Luis Enrique*

DID YOU KNOW?
Luis Enrique won gold at the Barcelona Olympics in 1992.

THIS PAGE: LUIS ENRIQUE - RELATIVE VETERAN WHO IS BEGINNING TO SHOW WORLD-CLASS FORM FOR BARCELONA AND SPAIN.

OPPOSITE PAGE: CUTTING INSIDE THE FAEROE ISLANDS DEFENCE IN SPAIN'S 3–1 FINAL QUALIFYING MATCH ON OCTOBER 10TH, 1997.

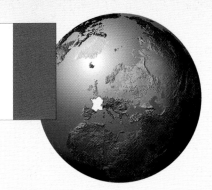

ATTACK
France
MAURICE

Since Jean-Pierre Papin, France has had trouble finding a consistent goalscorer. The host team will need to end the goal drought that has seen them fail to live up to expectations in all competitions this decade if they are to reach the latter stages of their own World Cup. So a nation's hopes are pinned on the promising start this young goal-poacher has made to his international career.

He learned his trade at Olympique Lyonnais, where he became a star of the Olympic team and the French under-21 side before a bright career looked jeopardized after he was side-lined for six months with an Achilles tendon injury sustained in a League match against Nantes. When fit, however, he was a regular scorer for the mid-table side before his move to PSG in the summer of 1997.

Working well off the ball, looking for space, this slight and unassuming striker is very quick on the ball and a clinical finisher. There's more to his game than just scoring goals, however. If he can't find a shooting chance himself, he has the ability and vision to set up teammates with chances.

Alain Giresse, a regular goalscorer in the great French team of the 1980s, speaks very highly of him. As does Roy Hodgson, the manager who took Switzerland to USA 94. After his appointment as coach at Inter Milan, Hodgson wasted no time in travelling to Lyon to see the most promising prospect of Olympique Lyonnais' excellent youth development programme.

The calmness with which the youngster took his goal for Lyonnais against Lazio in the 1996 UEFA Cup shows that he is not over-awed by the big occasion. However, he will be well aware that half of France believes their side will win on their own soil. To do that, they're going to need this newcomer to score goals. That's a lot to expect from a player who is still very inexperienced at international level. However, with his uncanny eye for goal and good teamwork, don't be surprised to see this relative unknown play a major part in France's bid for glory.

FULL NAME:
Florian Maurice
BORN:
20.1.74
BIRTHPLACE:
Sainte-Foy-Les-Lyon
HEIGHT:
1.75m/5ft 9in
WEIGHT:
73kg/11st 7lbs
CLUBS:
Olympique Lyonnais, PSG
DEBUT:
1997

❝ A born striker. ❞
— *Alain Giresse*

DID YOU KNOW?
Maurice was only one of ten homegrown players in the Lyon first-team squad of 1996/97.

THIS PAGE: SHOWING HIS DETERMINATION AGAINST ITALY'S FABIO CANNAVARO AT LE TOURNOI.

OPPOSITE PAGE: FLORIAN MAURICE LEAVES BRAZIL'S DUNGA FOR DEAD IN FRANCE'S 1–1 DRAW AT LE TOURNOI.

Cameroon
MBOMA

FULL NAME:
Patrick Mboma

BORN:
15.11.70

BIRTHPLACE:
Douala

HEIGHT:
1.85m/6ft 1in

WEIGHTT:
85kg/13st 5lbs

CLUBS:
Chateroux, Metz,
Paris Saint-Germain,
Gamba Osaka

DEBUT:
1993

> **66** I care about the
> **team victory, not my personal**
> **glory. 99**
> — *Patrick Mboma*

DID YOU KNOW?
Mboma's family emigrated to France
when he was two. He is a French
national but has chosen to play
his football for his motherland.

THIS PAGE: PATRICK MBOMA — STOOD OUT
IN AN IMPRESSIVE PERFORMANCE AGAINST
ENGLAND AT WEMBLEY LAST YEAR.

OPPOSITE PAGE: ONE OF AFRICA'S BEST
FORWARDS IN RECENT YEARS.

Patrick Mboma first became interested in football after watching the 1978 World Cup. That experience, he says, gave him his dream to play in a World Cup himself. Perhaps we all had the same dream. But this summer, after the disappointment of being dropped from the USA 94 squad, that dream will at last almost certainly come true for this on-form striker.

In France, both at Metz and during two spells at PSG, Mboma was never more than a squad player, kept out of the limelight by the likes of George Weah, David Ginola and Patrice Loko. He says he 'wasn't able to display his real ability' in France. 'I didn't have the trust of my manager.' Undoubtedly, this situation affected his international career prospects. In Osaka, however, he has become a superstar. While many players have previously gone to Japan to prolong their careers, Mboma's has flourished there. He scored his first ever top-class hat-trick in the annual J League All-Stars game in 1997, and then went on to score in six consecutive J-League games in August and September 1996. He has been banging them in for Gamba ever since.

The explosion of his career in Japan has given him a new chance in the national squad. He was recalled to the team for the qualifier against Togo in November 1996 and promptly scored. 'It started with the game against Namibia,' he recalls. 'After that I have been feeling so confident, I've really surprised myself.' That confidence got him two more goals against Namibia in a 4–0 African Nations Cup victory and another in Angola. He then secured Cameroon's qualification for France with a brace of blistering long-range efforts against Zimbabwe in Harare to finish as the overall top-scorer in the African section qualifying for France.

Mboma is an excellent athlete with great balance that allows him to stay on the ball under intense pressure. He is on fire for both club and country, and has demonstrated that he can also score from anywhere.

Yugoslavia
MIJATOVIC

Montenegrin playmaker-turned-sharp-shooter, Predrag Mijatovic is one of the men Yugoslavia are expecting to blast holes in the world's tightest defences this summer. His recent performances in attack at both club and international level suggest that he is more than capable of living up to these expectations. Impressive displays in front of goal for both Valencia and Real Madrid over the past three seasons have drawn rave reviews in the Spanish football press. The 28 Mijatovic goals that shot Valencia to a league runners-up spot in 1996 earned the Yugoslav the Spanish Footballer of the Year title that season. And now 'Pedje', as the Spaniards call him, is doing the business at international level as well.

The £6.3 million striker, signed two seasons ago by then Real Madrid coach Fabio Capello to partner Croatian striker Davor Suker (see page 85), belted a hat-trick inside 25 minutes as Yugoslavia clouted Hungary 7–1 in the away leg of their World Cup play-off. He then followed that up with a further four goals as Yugoslavia again trounced the Hungarians 5–0 at home in the return leg. Earlier in the qualifying campaign, his six strikes (including winning goals at home and away against Euro 96 runners-up the Czech Republic) as well as a late equalizer in Budapest against eventual automatic qualifiers Spain, had served to carry Yugoslavia into a comfortable second-place in Group 6 and earned them a play-off place.

A lightning-fast and very stylish footballer, Mijatovic's guile and invention are the perfect complement to the more graceful approach work of his strike partner Dejan Savicevic (see page 74). He is, however, occasionally prone to take a tumble in and around the box, a habit that has prompted the outspoken Atletico Madrid president Jesus Gil to ironically accuse the striker of being an 'epileptic'. Not one to accept criticism lightly, nor to excuse or deny the existence of this aspect of his game, Mijatovic responded: 'It's only jealousy. Anyway, it takes real skill to be a good actor!'

FULL NAME:
Predrag Mijatovic
BORN:
19.1.69
BIRTHPLACE:
Podgorica
HEIGHT:
1.77m/5ft 10in
WEIGHT:
75kg/11st 11lbs
CLUBS:
Partizan Belgrade, Valencia, Real Madrid
DEBUT:
1989

❝ We prepared for the play-off with Hungary as though we were about to meet Brazil. Now we will be the wonder of France. ❞
— *Predrag Mijatovic*

DID YOU KNOW?
Coach Fabio Capello remarked during his spell at Real Madrid that he 'wouldn't swap Mijatovic for Ronaldo'.

THIS PAGE: PREDRAG MIJATOVIC — A VERSATILE PERFORMER WITH AN EYE FOR GOAL.

OPPOSITE PAGE: MIJATOVIC HAS BROUGHT RENEWED FLAIR TO REAL MADRID'S ATTACK.

Denmark
MOLNAR

FULL NAME:
Miklos Molnar

BORN:
10.4.70

BIRTHPLACE:
Copenhagen

HEIGHT:
1.80m/ 5ft 11in

WEIGHT:
80kg/12st 8lbs

CLUBS:
Standard Liege, Servette,
St Etienne, Frankfurt, Lyngby,
Herfolge BK, Seville

DEBUT:
1990

Denmark's most recent goalscoring sensation has been around a bit in European football and made his international debut way back in 1990. He had become the Danish league's most consistent goalscorer before his move to Spain last summer, but only after his recent spate of extraordinarily prolific goalscoring in his home country has he established himself as a first choice in the national team. Nevertheless, he is now beginning to show the same nose for goal for this highly rated Danish national team as he has done at club level.

In the qualifying game at home to Bosnia, he was brought on as substitute during the dying moments of the match. The Danes were already a goal up thanks to defender Marc Rieper, and the Bosnians were looking panicky in defence as they tried to clear a last minute attack. Molnar sensed their insecurity and harassed them until they eventually gave him the ball in a dangerous position. That was all the striker needed and he calmly slotted the ball home to secure a 2-0 victory. It was a coolly taken goal of the kind he had been scoring week in and week out in the league, but the calmness with which he accepted his chance belied the fact that it was his first goal for his country.

He followed that up with the goal that gave the Danes a 3-0 half time lead over Croatia after Brian and Michael Laudrup (see pages 46 and 49) had given them an early cushion. Denmark went on to win that game 3-1, demonstrating that they are looking to add to their European Championship success of 1992.

Denmark are not short of classy attackers by any means, but Miklos Molnar is their most potent force at the moment. He has shown himself to be confident enough to perform at international level, and now, at last, the man astutely contracted to Seville until the year 2000 looks set to become a household name around the world.

66 My work is in the last
16 metres. **99**
— *Miklos Molnar*

DID YOU KNOW?
Molnar's get-out clause from his contract at Seville is set at over £10m.

THIS PAGE: MIKLOS MOLNAR — NOW
PLAYING HIS CLUB FOOTBALL IN SPAIN,
THE STRIKER IS ON THE BRINK OF
INTERNATIONAL STARDOM.

OPPOSITE PAGE: IN ACTION FOR DENMARK
AS HE ESTABLISHES HIS PLACE IN THE TEAM.

Spain
'ALFONSO' MUNOZ

That Spain's only major international tournament success to date is the European Championships of 1964 is surprising in a nation of 36 million people with such a proud footballing tradition at club level. In recent years, most of the blame for this under-achievement has been put down to their failure to produce a natural goalscorer in a league dominated by imported attackers. It is reasonable then, for the Spanish to be expecting a lot from this young striker who came so close to becoming *pichichi* (the League's top scorer) in 1997.

At Betis, Alfonso plays in a slightly retarded position behind the main striker, preferring to attack defenders from the right-hand side of the pitch with the ball at his feet. In the absence of Julio Salinas, whose international career was extended beyond his usefulness at club level chiefly because he was the team's only reliable goalscorer, he is likely to be given a more advance role, most probably as a solitary striker playing in front of an attack-minded five-man midfield.

Alfonso is an instinctive goal-getter who only ever has one thing on his mind when bearing down on a goalkeeper, but whether or not he can adapt to the role of target man, rather than playing in his preferred deeper position, stalking the edge of the area, has yet to be proved. But with the likes of Raul Gonzalez Blanco (see page 26) looking a world-class act, Spain now have the strongest team the country has put together for a long time and look perfectly capable of taking the trophy home with them.

A lot rides on the performances of this Euro 96 squad member. No team that looks so weak in attack as Spain without their new centre-forward could ever win the World Cup, but if the young striker from Madrid, who plays his football in the Seville club Real Betis, can add to the five goals he scored in qualification and live up to the expectations his country have for him, he could prove the unlikely key to their first ever World Cup success.

FULL NAME:	Alfonso Perez Muñoz
BORN:	26.9.72
BIRTHPLACE:	Madrid
HEIGHT:	1.72m/5ft 8in
WEIGHT:	69kg/10st 12lbs
CLUBS:	Real Betis
DEBUT:	1992

❝ He's the best centre-forward we've got. ❞
— *national coach Javier Clemente*

DID YOU KNOW?
Alfonso began this season with two goals against BVSC Budapest in the European Cup Winners' Cup.

THIS PAGE: ALFONSO — IS THE REAL BETIS STRIKER TO BECOME THE MATADOR HIS COUNTRY NEEDS?

OPPOSITE PAGE: CONTROL AND BALANCE... AND AN EYE FOR GOAL.

FULL NAME:
Luc Nilis

BORN:
25.5.67

BIRTHPLACE:
Hasselt

HEIGHT:
1.85m/6ft 1in

WEIGHT:
76kg/12st

CLUBS:
FC Halvenweg Zonhoven,
Winterslag, Anderlecht,
PSV Eindhoven

DEBUT:
1988

66 **The sort of forward who can turn the course of a game with one single moment of brilliance.** 99
— *national coach
Lorenzo Staelens*

DID YOU KNOW?
A former coach believed Nilis 'didn't have the self-belief to make it at international level'.

THIS PAGE: LUC NILIS — DEVASTATINGLY EFFECTIVE IN FRONT OF GOAL.

OPPOSITE PAGE: THE PSV PLAYER IS AT THE TOP OF HIS FORM AT CLUB LEVEL.

L eeds United supporters will remember Nilis well. He was the man who scored twice against the Yorkshire club in the last seven minutes to give PSV Eindhoven a 5–3 victory in the enthralling UEFA Cup second round clash between the clubs in October 1995, after the English side had valiantly fought back to 3–3 from 3–1 down at the break. Werder Bremen fans will also recall the last-minute winner that put their club out in the following round. Indeed, Holland's top league scorer in 1996, with 21 goals, has been a consistently prolific striker throughout the career which took him to the very top of Belgian football with Anderlecht before his move to his current club in July 1994.

Such a record at domestic level has made him hard to leave out of the national team, but his record at international level is not quite so impressive. He took no fewer than 22 games to score his first goal for Belgium and has hardly been prolific since, managing only six goals in his first 40 appearances. But the reason he is still selected, and the reason he was given so long to prove himself in the national side in the first place, is that apart from his goalscoring prowess at club level, he is also one of the better football players the Belgian national team have at their disposal. Nilis has a wonderful first touch and once he has the ball firmly under control at his feet, he becomes a highly skilful and dangerous striker who, as his coach puts it, 'twists and turns past defenders as though they weren't there'.

And as long as Luis Oliveira keeps scoring, Belgians won't worry that Nilis still hasn't found his scoring boots at international level. The PSV player is just as useful to his team as a provider of goals as he is as a goalscorer, and with the likes of Enzo Scifo (see page 77) still creating chances, the Belgians will come south across the border fancying their chances at France 98.

ATTACK
Austria
POLSTER

Austria's leading goalscorer of all time continues to lead the line for his country with the same vigour he brought to the international stage in 1982. Polster scored on his debut against Turkey, and has been Austria's first-choice centre forward almost ever since. Another glut of goals in qualifying for France 98 has seen him inch ever nearer the 40-goal mark for Austria, and further clear of Hans Krankl's next-best international tally of 32.

A tall, gangly targetman, 'Toni' Polster started his professional domestic career with Austria Vienna over 15 years ago. His constantly improving strike-rate during five seasons with the club peaked in 1986/87 when he hit the net a stunning 39 times to win the European Golden Boot. That record prompted a lucrative transfer to Torino, the now fallen giants of Italian football, where he looked the perfect signing when he scored on his Serie A debut.

But like so many strikers who are bought on the strength of a goalscoring purple patch, Polster struggled to sustain this incredible form and spent just a year in Italy before leaving for Seville. This turned out to be the right choice. Concerns that he wasn't up to the job at the very highest level were soon forgotten as he banged in another astonishing record of 33 League goals in 1989/90. He also propelled Austria to the Italia 90 finals with a last-game hat-trick against East Germany. Once again. Polster returned to Italy billed as a potential superstar... and once again he failed to live up to expectations, failing to score as Austria lost meekly to the hosts and Czechoslovakia.

Now playing his football in Germany after spells at two other Spanish clubs, Polster's star is again in the ascendancy. He is approaching the same international form he showed when he scored 10 goals in six European Championship qualifiers in 1994/95. It was his prolific record of a strike every other game that went a long way to helping Austria through their qualifying group.

FULL NAME:
Anton Polster

BORN:
10.3.64

BIRTHPLACE:
Vienna

HEIGHT:
1.86m/6ft 1in

WEIGHT:
84kg/13st 3lbs

CLUBS:
Austria Vienna, Torino, Sevilla, Logrones, Rayo Vallecano, Cologne

DEBUT:
1982

66 **Thanks to recent developments (the Bosman ruling) our team will be stronger by 20 per cent.** 99
— *Anton Polster*

DID YOU KNOW?
Despite scoring just nine times for Torino, Polster posted Serie A's only hat-trick of the 1987/88 season, against Sampdoria.

THIS PAGE: ANTON POLSTER — THE UNDOUBTED KING OF AUSTRIAN FOOTBALL.

OPPOSITE PAGE: THE EXPERIENCED FRONTMAN EVADES A DEFENDER'S DESPERATE LUNGE.

FULL NAME:
Fabrizio Ravanelli

BORN:
11.12.68

BIRTHPLACE:
Perugia

HEIGHT:
1.88m/6ft 2in

WEIGHT:
85kg/13st 5lbs

CLUBS:
Perugia, Avellino, Reggiana,
Juventus, Middlesbrough,
Marseille

DEBUT:
1995

Even when he was at Juventus, the 'White Feather' was often considered a 'journeyman footballer', good enough, but never outstanding, and never really in line for international greatness. He could score goals, that was never in doubt, but his approach play was thought to be inferior to those around him, and he was perceived as a hard-running workhorse who was most useful to the team when they didn't have the ball.

Indeed, Ravanelli didn't make his international debut until he was 26, and was later omitted from the national team right up until the World Cup play-off match in Russia, autumn 1997. The decision to play him in the Russia game was probably made as a result of Filippo Inzaghi's less than impressive performance against England in Rome in the previous match, when the striker was substituted at half time, as well as the momentary loss of international form of Gianfranco Zola (see page 93).

Ravanelli is quick in front of goal, strong in the air and in the tackle, can shield the ball well and has a dynamite left foot. But beyond all these footballing qualities, he is a charismatic figure in any team he plays for, a character who can lift the level of performance of those around him. For this reason, as much as for his recently acquired experience of football in England and France, Ravanelli's recent return to the Italian team might be more permanent this time round.

Middlesbrough fans will remember the combination of Ravanelli and Juninho (see page 136) as the outstanding partnership in the team that reached the finals of both the FA Cup and English League Cup in the same extraordinary season that the Teesside club somehow managed to get themselves relegated. Ravanelli has since moved on, and Boro fans were largely pleased to see the back of him. They knew that he never wanted to leave Juve, and felt that this could be seen in his level of commitment to the club. But head physio Bob Ward tells a different story. He was immediately impressed by Ravanelli's application to his fitness and called him 'the perfect professional'.

> **66 An international left foot with a Sunday morning right foot. 99**
> — *Boro fanzine*

DID YOU KNOW?
Ravanelli scored a hat-trick against Liverpool on his home debut for Middlesbrough.

THIS PAGE: FABRIZIO RAVANELLI — ALWAYS RESPECTED AS A PLAYER, HIS OUTSPOKEN NATURE HAS MADE ENEMIES OFF THE PITCH.

OPPOSITE PAGE: THE 'WHITE FEATHER' CHASES THE BALL ON HIS RETURN TO THE NATIONAL TEAM.

ATTACK
Brazil
ROMARIO

Full name:
Romario de Souza Farias

Born:
29.1.66

Birthplace:
Rio de Janeiro

Height:
1.65m/5ft 3in

Weight
70kg/11st

Clubs:
Vasco da Gama, PSV, Barcelona, Flamengo, Valencia

Debut:
1986

International honours:
World Cup winner 1994, Copa America winner 1989, 1997

66 **God created me to delight people with my goals.** **99**
— *Romario*

DID YOU KNOW?
Romario's favourite pastime is beach volleyball.

THIS PAGE: ROMARIO — A DROP OF THE SHOULDER AND A LIGHTNING BURST OF PACE TAKE THE BRAZILIAN PAST ANOTHER DEFENDER.

OPPOSITE PAGE: WHAT HAPPENS NEXT? YOU GUESSED IT. ROMARIO SCORES FOR BRAZIL.

Now overshadowed by the media attention surrounding Ronaldo (see page 71), it should be remembered that it was the smaller half of Brazil's *dupla Ro-Ro* striking partnership who scored in every match of USA 94 – including the World Cup Final penalty shoot-out. Romario has had a torrid four years since then, during which he didn't play for Brazil for two and a half years.

In 1994, as a Barcelona player and FIFA's Player of the Year, he was criticized by the Nou Camp faithful for apathy and returned home to play for Flamengo that winter. Back in Rio, he separated from his wife, Monica Santoro; his team had a poor two seasons, and he was subsequently off-loaded to Valencia on loan. There, he lost his first-team place, went back to Flamengo, was injured in his first game and saw his side go out of another Brazilian Championship. During that time, he was known not to turn up for training and once pulled out of the international squad for personal reasons. This action angered national coach Mario Zagallo, not least because it was remembered that as a teenager, Romario had been kicked out of the World Youth Championships for breaking a curfew.

He claims that a visit to a mystic healer at the Japanese Messianic Church in Rio 'cleansed and balanced' him. His psychic energy re-attuned to the Universe, he scored a hat-trick in his next match against Botafogo. A further 17 goals in 11 games during the Rio/São Paolo tournament won him his international recall, and he took his second chance with a man-of-the-match performance in the 4–2 win over Poland.

His return has been made not by playing the offside line and picking up on defensive slips as he always used to, but by operating from the deeper role he developed at Flamengo. From there, he can avoid his markers and find more space to serve Ronaldo with his immaculate passing.

He is blessed with a rare precision of touch and the pace over a few metres which leaves defenders rooted to the spot. His coach at Flamengo, the ex-international star Junior, says: 'I have no doubt that Romario could play another World Cup in this new position.'

He has married again, to Daniela Favato, has a child, a full-time contract at Valencia and is likely to figure prominently in France 98.

ATTACK
Brazil
RONALDO

The young man who Pelé (see page 13) has called 'an exquisite footballer' will be the biggest star of the team most likely to be the first ever to come from another continent and retain the World Cup. Although he is not known for holding up the ball and bringing others into play, when he has the ball at his feet, few defenders would deny that this 21-year-old has already become the best striker of his generation, if not of all time.

Spotted playing beach football by Social Ramos Club (after Flamengo had refused to pay his bus fare to training!), he then went to play for second division San Cristavão. His performances for them in the Indoor League prompted the legendary Jairzhino (see page 94) to persuade Cruzeiro of Belo Horizonte to sign the 15-year-old. There he scored 54 goals in 54 games before following in Romario's (see page 68) footsteps to PSV Eindhoven in Holland. Two seasons and 30 goals later, and after coach Dick Advocaat had left him on the bench following an injury, he became a millionaire overnight by netting 15% of his £13m transfer fee to Barcelona.

He repaid Barcelona with a club-record 34 league goals over the 1996/97 season, before repaying his agent Giovanni Branchini by signing for Inter Milan – where Branchini has offices – at the beginning of the 1997-98 season. There, he is reputed to earn £2m a year in wages plus nearly another £1m annually from his sponsors. His transfer fee may reach an astonishing £82m if he stays the full nine years of his contract.

As powerful in the air as he is on the ground, he regularly brushes aside the best defenders with a deadly combination of strength and pace as he continues his relentless and direct charge towards goal – and one-on-one with the keeper, his finishing is invariably cool. His coach at Barcelona, Bobby Robson, has said: 'You can go anywhere in the world and you won't find a player who can score goals like Ronaldo. He can pick the ball up anywhere and turn that into a goalscoring situation on his own. He is simply sensational.' In a crucial 1997 Spanish league match, the Deportivo defence resorted to bringing him down in the centre circle, only to see him regain his feet and score the winning goal that kept Barcelona in the title chase. He is perfectly capable of doing exactly the same thing at France 98.

FULL NAME:
Ronaldo Luiz Nazario da Lima

BORN:
22.9.76

BIRTHPLACE
Bento Ribeiro,
Rio de Janeiro

HEIGHT:
1.80m/5ft 11in

WEIGHT:
81kg/12st 11lbs

CLUBS:
Social Ramos, San Cristavão,
Cruzeiro, PSV Eindhoven,
Barcelona, Inter Milan

DEBUT:
1994

HONOURS:
World Cup winner 1994,
Copa America winner 1997

❝...he's still not a great team player; too obsessed with scoring great individual goals. ❞
— *Roberto Carlos*

DID YOU KNOW?
Ronaldo was a member of the USA 94 squad, but did not play at the finals.

THIS PAGE: RONALDO — OR RONALDINHO AS HE'S KNOWN IN SOUTH AMERICA, LIFTS THE COPA AMERICA.

OPPOSITE PAGE: HE'S INSIDE THE AREA AND CARLOS GAMARRA IS BEATEN. GOALKEEPER CHILAVERT IS IN TROUBLE.

A T T A C K
Chile
SALAS

Marcelo Salas is one of the most exciting prospects to come out of South America for decades. A striker with an absolutely phenomenal goalscoring record, he has already outgrown the tag of being the 'new Ivan Zamorano' (see page 90) and looks like being the star of this Chilean team for many years to come.

The 'Matador' began his career at Santos, a local amateur side in Temuco, and made the break into top-level football at the beginning of 1994. He immediately made his mark by scoring for Universidad de Chile on his debut, a feat he would later repeat both for River Plate and for the national team. He scored a total of 90 goals for the 'U' before making the trip across the Andes in September 1996 to play for River Plate in Buenos Aires. There, it took him less than a minute to register his debut goal against rivals Boca Juniors. Subsequent strikes helped River to the Apertura Championship that year, by which time Salas had firmly established himself as the first choice to partner Ivan Zamorano in the Chilean attack.

By last summer, Salas was beginning to attract some serious attention from European clubs, with Napoli and Juventus among those interested in him. But there were other players in the River Plate squad that president Alfredo Davicce was more willing to lose, and he declared that the club was not prepared to let Salas go for 'less than 20 million US dollars'. However, when Manchester United moved for Salas last autumn, coach Alex Ferguson said the transfer fee was not important. The English club had been foiled in their attempts to get a work permit for the Brazilian international Celio Silva during the summer, and believed that the Chilean striker would make a tremendous addition to an already awesome squad.

But as Andy Cole returned to goalscoring form for Manchester United, the club chose to end the lengthy drawn-out negotiations with River Plate without clinching the deal. At the time of going to press, Salas looked set to further his career in in Italy.

FULL NAME:
Marcelo Salas

BORN:
24.12.74

BIRTHPLACE:
Temuco

HEIGHT:
1.74m/5ft 9in

WEIGHT:
75kg/12st 4lbs

CLUBS:
Universidad de Chile, River Plate

DEBUT:
1994

❝ I've got my feet on the ground. ❞
— Marcelo Salas on his impending move to Europe

DID YOU KNOW?
Napoli had a 12million US dollar offer for Salas turned down by River Plate last year.

THIS PAGE: MARCELO SALAS — COULD BECOME ONE OF SOUTH AMERICA'S GREATEST EVER STRIKERS.

OPPOSITE PAGE: SALAS IN ACTION AGAINST THE USA.

Yugoslavia
SAVICEVIC

FULL NAME:
Dejan Savicevic

BORN:
15.9.66

BIRTHPLACE:
Podgorica

HEIGHT:
1.79m/5ft 10in

WEIGHT:
78kg/12st 4lbs

CLUBS:
OJK Titograd, Buducnost,
Red Star Belgrade, AC Milan

DEBUT:
1986

Seven goals in Yugoslavia's successful qualifying campaign have given Dejan Savicevic a guaranteed first-team place in his country's team for this, his second World Cup appearance. This wonderfully creative frontman, who shows an outstandingly deft touch in and around the penalty area, has come a long way since Italia 90, when his team was eventually eliminated in the quarter-finals after a penalty shoot-out against Argentina.

Having helped Red Star Belgrade to European Cup Final glory over Marseille in 1991, Savicevic was bought by AC Milan for a staggering £12 million in the 1992 close season. Incredibly, he failed to hold down a first-team place at the San Siro for two years, kept out of the team by the Dutch genius Marco van Basten, the Italian international Gianluigi Lentini and France's strike sensation of the time, Jean-Pierre Papin. But when the Yugoslav was eventually granted the chance to justify his huge price tag, he carved out a place in AC Milan legend. Called up late into the *Rossoneri*'s 1993/94 European Champions League campaign, his man-of-the-match display in the final utterly upstaged Barcelona's star man Hristo Stoichkov (see page 82) and carried his club to a monumental 4–0 win.

AC Milan have preferred to use him as a midfielder, which goes a long way towards explaining a relatively poor return of only seven goals in his last two seasons with the club, but Savicevic has been playing in attack for Yugoslavia. There, he has been employed for much of his country's qualifying programme for France 98 as part of a three-pronged attack alongside Predrag Mijatovic (see page 57) and another of his old Red Star teammates, Dragan Stojkovic. The trio have proved themselves to be one of the most dangerous attacking forces in international football, not least in the 12–1 aggregate demolition of Hungary in the play-offs. The 31-year-old AC Milan player is responding to the more advanced position he adopts for Yugoslavia by playing some of the best football of his illustrious career.

> **❝It was Savicevic's quality that made the difference. ❞**
> — *coach Slobodan Santrac after defeating Hungary in the play-offs*

DID YOU KNOW?
Dragan Ciric, Barcelona's 23-year-old signing from Partizan Belgrade, is being touted by the Yugoslav press as the 'new Savicevic'.

THIS PAGE: DEJAN SAVICEVIC – HIS GOALS IN QUALIFYING HAVE TAKEN YUGOSLAVIA TO FRANCE.

OPPOSITE PAGE: SAVICEVIC STRUGGLES TO REACH THE BALL IN ACTION FOR HIS COUNTRY.

Belgium
SCIFO

Belgium's brilliant playmaker could be considered a victim of his own success. He gained his first international cap when he was just 18 while at Anderlecht in the mid-1980s. His mercurial skills set his club on course to three successive Belgian League titles in 1985, 1986 and 1987 before he elected to further his career in the country of his ancestry.

At that time there was no stopping him, and many people thought the young midfielder, as he was then, could become one of the greatest footballers of all time. He has an incredibly precise first touch, which his team employs to great effect in fast counter-attacking moves, and he quickly became a pivotal figure in the national team. But leaving his homeland at such a tender age proved rather too much for the youngster, and he has since struggled to live up to the lofty expectations made of him when he was first an Anderlecht player. Scifo's adventures outside Belgium were largely uneventful, and he returned there a year ago having missed most of Monaco's 1996/97 season through injury. Now that he is back at home, though, his form is improving again. That is good for such a proud club as Anderlecht, who re-signed Scifo after finishing the 1996/97 season well off the pace in fourth place. And it is also good news for the national side, for whom Scifo is beginning to combine well with on-form striker Luis Oliveira in the build-up to France.

Belgium are rarely a fancied team at the World Cup, and were well beaten into second place by neighbours Holland in qualifying for France before scraping through their play-off matches against the Republic of Ireland. But once they're at the World Cup Finals, they tend to reach the knock-out stages. If Scifo can set up his front runners with goalscoring opportunities, he may well be able to forget the disappointment of going out to a last-minute David Platt goal against England in 1990. Perhaps this time he can lead his team as far as the semi-finals, just as he did way back in 1986.

FULL NAME:
Enzo Scifo

BORN:
19.2.66

BIRTHPLACE:
Haine-Saint-Paul

HEIGHT:
1.85m/6ft 1in

WEIGHT:
80kg/12st 8lbs

CLUBS:
La Louviere, Anderlecht, Inter Milan, Bordeaux, Auxerre, Torino, Monaco, Anderlecht

DEBUT:
1984

66 If you give Enzo total licence to run the game as he sees fit, the results can be spectacular. **99**
— *Guy Roux, former coach at Auxerre*

DID YOU KNOW?
Scifo won the Belgian League in three successive years in his first spell with Anderlecht.

THIS PAGE: ENZO SCIFO — THE MAVERICK GENIUS OF BELGIUM'S IMPRESSIVE SIDE.

OPPOSITE PAGE: THE BELGIANS FACE NEIGHBOURS HOLLAND IN THE FIRST ROUND, AS THEY DID IN QUALIFYING. THEY WILL NEED SCIFO AT HIS BEST IF THEY ARE TO MAKE THE SECOND ROUND.

England
SHEARER

FULL NAME:
Alan Shearer

BORN:
13.8.70

BIRTHPLACE:
Newcastle

HEIGHT:
1.80m/5ft 11in

WEIGHT:
71kg/11st 3lbs

CLUBS:
Southampton, Blackburn Rovers,
Newcastle United

DEBUT:
1992

66 When I'm on a football pitch
it's serious business and
I want to win. **99**
— Alan Shearer

DID YOU KNOW?
The defender he most fears is
Arsenal's Tony Adams
(see page 170).

THIS PAGE: ALAN SHEARER — NORMALLY
IT'S JUST THE ONE HAND ALOFT TO
CELEBRATE A GOAL, BUT THIS WAS IN A
WORLD CUP QUALIFIER AND TWO ARE
JUSTIFIED.

OPPOSITE PAGE: ENGLAND'S NEW NUMBER
NINE HAS PROVED A MORE THAN ADEQUATE
REPLACEMENT FOR GARY LINEKER.

When this 15-year-old son of a sheet metal worker left the North East to begin his career with Southampton, Newcastle United let £15m slip through their fingers. Shearer eventually signed professional terms with the South Coast club in April 1988. While the 23 goals he scored in the two seasons he was there were not what kept the Saints up, he showed that there was a lot more to his game than simply goals. His touch is confident, his passing clean and his crosses from the right are as good as any winger's. He sets up as many goals as he scores, and while Ronaldo (see page 71) may be a better marksman, Shearer is a complete player who would not look out of place in any position on the football pitch.

The emerging talent at Southampton was soon recognized by newly rich Blackburn Rovers and they were prepared to break the bank to get their man. The £3.3m Blackburn manager Kenny Dalglish paid for Shearer in 1993 was at that time a British record fee. Shearer proved that he was worth the outlay by getting 112 goals in 140 appearances and the Premiership Championship in 1995. By the time Shearer went back home in 1996, he was valued at £15m, a world record fee at the time that has only recently been surpassed by the sum Real Betis paid for the Brazilian sensation Denilson (see page 118).

His remarkable goalscoring record at club level has not always transferred to the international arena, however. Before qualification for France began, he was only averaging a goal every four games for his country. Indeed, when he scored against Switzerland at Euro 96, it was his first for over 1,000 minutes of international football, but he immediately followed that up with strikes against Scotland, Holland and Germany and is now as likely to score for England as he for his club.

Shearer missed the early part of the 97/98 season through injury and England qualified for France without him, but coach Glenn Hoddle will want to call on the services of the PFA's 1995 Player of the Year if the English are to challenge for their second World Cup victory.

With his slight frame and youthful features, he hardly looks a lethal striker, but the 'baby-faced assassin' has made a sensational start as a goalscorer in the English Premiership following his £1.5m move from Molde in July 1996. Manchester United coach Alex Ferguson knew the pedigree of a player who had scored four goals in his first five internationals, but he did not expect his new £1.5m signing to make such an immediate impact in the team.

Nevertheless, the pre-season form of the young Norwegian was good enough for him to be brought off the bench as a substitute during the visit of Blackburn Rovers in August 1997. He was Manchester United's best player that day. He created a number of chances for himself and for his teammates, capping his performance by scoring a well-taken goal after goalkeeper Tim Flowers had parried his first shot. In that game, he launched himself into the starting line-up for 33 games at his new club in his first season at Old Trafford. He scored a further 17 times that year to help Manchester United win the Premiership title.

Although he lacks the build of many Premiership strikers, he has pace, quick feet and fast enough reactions to more than compensate for this. He can be pushed off the ball by players more physical than he is, but they have to catch him first. More often that not, they don't get near him as he uses his great ball skills to twist and turn his way out of trouble. He rarely has an off day and his hard running and workrate have made him a favourite at Old Trafford. As have his goals.

Solskjaer joined Clausengen in 1989 and played five full seasons there before moving to Molde in 1995. He broke in to the Norwegian squad while he was still playing for Molde but has yet to confirm himself as a first-choice striker for his national side. However, a second season of the same form as he showed in his first year in England will make it hard for the Norwegians to leave him out of the side for France.

FULL NAME:
Ole Gunnar Solskjaer

BORN:
26.2.73

BIRTHPLACE:
Kristiansund

HEIGHT:
1.80m/5ft 10in

WEIGHT:
73kg/11st 8lbs

CLUBS:
FK Clausengen, Molde, Manchester United

DEBUT:
1995

> 66 He reminds me of Denis Law. 99
> — *former teammate Eric Cantona*

DID YOU KNOW?
Solskjaer's father is a champion wrestler.

THIS PAGE: OLE GUNNAR SOLSKJAER — HIS PERFORMANCES AT CLUB LEVEL HAVE DEMANDED HIS INCLUSION IN THE NORWEGIAN TEAM.

OPPOSITE PAGE: THE NORWEGIANS ARE NOTORIOUS FOR PLAYING THE LONG-BALL GAME, BUT AS MANCHESTER UNITED FANS WILL KNOW, SOLSKJAER BELIES THIS IMAGE.

Bulgaria
STOICHKOV

FULL NAME:
Hristo Stoichkov

BORN:
8.2.66

BIRTHPLACE:
Plovdiv

HEIGHT:
1.78m/5ft 10in

WEIGHT:
75kg/11st 11lbs

CLUBS:
Maritza Plovdiv, USM,
Youri Gagarine, Hebros, CSKA,
Barcelona, Parma, Barcelona

DEBUT:
1987

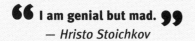

66 I am genial but mad. **99**
— *Hristo Stoichkov*

DID YOU KNOW?
The inhabitants of the village near Plovdiv where he was born have voted to change the name of their town to Stoichkovo.

THIS PAGE: HRISTO STOICHKOV — ARGUABLY BULGARIA'S GREATEST EVER PLAYER.

OPPOSITE PAGE: STOICHKOV HAS ONE OF THE MOST POWERFUL LEFT FEET IN THE BUSINESS.

Barcelona's unpredictable striker finished joint top scorer on six goals with Russia's Oleg Salenko at USA 94 and scored all three of Bulgaria's goals at Euro 96. When he is on form, which isn't always, he is one of the best inside-lefts playing today. He is also one of the game's more controversial figures.

Stoichkov first got into the CSKA team as an 18-year-old. A year later, he was banned for life for his part in the 1985 Bulgarian Cup Final brawl, but was reinstated less than a year after that incident. In his six seasons at CSKA, he scored 81 goals in 119 appearances for the club before moving to Barcelona for a Bulgarian record transfer fee of £2m.

In his first spell in Spanish football, he became a folk hero in Catalonia and the talisman of the Barcelona team that won the Spanish League on four consecutive occasions and the European Cup in 1994. In that same year, he played in the World Cup, was made European Footballer of the Year and was recognized at home as Bulgarian Sportsman of the Year.

But his temper remains his, and everybody else's, worst enemy. He was sent off no less than 11 times in his first six-year stint at Barcelona, and has on many occasions shown little respect for the other players on the pitch. He has admitted subjecting France's Marcel Desailly (see page 182) to racial abuse during the clash between the two countries at St James Park at Euro 96, and could only say that he hoped the Milan defender would 'take it like a man'.

He moved to Italy in 1995, but his yearning for his adopted homeland meant that he spent only one season at Parma before going back to Barcelona. Since returning, Barcelona and Stoichkov have failed to reach the heights they achieved under Johan Cruyff, but the Bulgarian has added one further club medal to his collection, coming on as a substitute in the 1–0 win over PSG in the 1997 European Cup Winners' Cup Final. He is still Bulgaria's best player.

ATTACK
Croatia
SUKER

Davor Suker, as Danish fans – and their goalkeeper Peter Schmeichel (see page 244) in particular – already know, is a world class striker who cannot be contained anywhere in his opponents' half of the pitch. He will always be remembered throughout Europe for that glorious chip over the Danish goalkeeper's giant frame that sealed a 3–1 victory for Croatia over the impressive defending champions at Euro 96. Earlier in that same game, it was a Suker long ball to Mario Stanic that caused his teammate to be brought down in the area for a penalty from which Suker scored. It was also a Suker pass that set up Zvonimir Boban (see page 109) for the second goal and the left-footed striker very nearly capped a quite wonderful individual performance with a brilliant shot from inside the centre-circle.

That was only one game, of course, and although he also scored against Germany in England that summer, it is fair to say that in his country's first encounter of Euro 96 against Turkey, Suker had looked anything but world class. But his overall record for Croatia of nearly a goal a game in more than a quarter century of appearances speaks for itself. Suker was already a household name among football fans the world over before Euro 96. He had first made a real name for himself in his homeland when he became the top scorer in the victorious 1987 under-18 World Championships, underlining that performance by becoming the Yugoslav League's top scorer while still playing for Osijek.

Since then he has become a hero in Spain, or at least in the cities of Seville and Madrid, and has been hitting the net with frightening regularity for both club and country. There is no reason to suppose that he won't do the same for Croatia at France 98 however much opposition defenders and coaches already know about him. He is very determined on the ball, and whenever he gets within range (and that means about 40 metres out), he only ever has one thing on his mind, to score or to set up a teammate to score.

FULL NAME:
Davor Suker
BORN:
1.1.68
BIRTHPLACE:
Osijek
HEIGHT:
1.83m/6ft
WEIGHT:
78kg/12st 4lbs
CLUBS:
Osijek, Dinamo Zagreb (now FC Croatia), Seville, Real Madrid
DEBUT:
1990

66 Suker is hard to cover because he often disappears behind the defence and then pops up suddenly further forward. **99**
— *Peter Schmeichel*

DID YOU KNOW?
Suker is Croatia's top goalscorer.

THIS PAGE: DAVOR SUKER — OTHERWISE KNOWN AS 'SUKERMAN'.

OPPOSITE PAGE: SUKER DISPLAYS CONTROL AND VISION IN THE RED-AND-WHITE CHECKS OF CROATIA.

Italy
VIALLI

FULL NAME:
Gianluca Vialli

BORN:
9.7.64

BIRTHPLACE:
Cremona

HEIGHT:
1.80m/5ft 11in

WEIGHT:
85kg/13st 5lbs

CLUBS:
Cremonese, Sampdoria, Juventus, Chelsea

DEBUT:
1985

Italy's shaven-headed 1995 Player of the Year started out in 1984 as a curly-haired teenage winger whose outspoken views gave him as much coverage in the Italian football press as his sensational football. A high-profile move to Sampdoria four years later brought him a European Cup Winners' Cup medal, three Italian cups and the league title, as his partnership with Roberto Mancini blossomed into the most feared attacking force in Serie A. During this time, he became an international regular and the golden boy of Italian football.

But everything went wrong after a £12m transfer to Juve in 1992. Vialli scored only six goals in his first season in Turin, while a knee injury kept him out for most of the following year, and a dispute with former national coach Arrigo Sacchi caused Vialli to vow that he would never play for Italy again. Concentrating on his club football, he then won the league with Juve in 1995 and European Cup in 1996 before moving to London to play under Ruud Gullit.

Although Vialli was signed by Chelsea as a first-choice striker, he soon found himself on the bench. But whenever he has come into the team, he has shown glimpses of the skills that have earned him recognition as a world-class striker. He marked his first full appearance for Chelsea in 1996 with four goals, and must have been very disappointed not to find himself in the starting line-up the following week.

The problem for Vialli at Chelsea is similar to that at international level and is linked to the sweeper system both teams employ. There are only two forward positions available, and until Vialli develops an understanding of the kind he had with Mancini, he is unlikely to become a Chelsea regular. And without regular action at club level, his chances of playing in the World Cup this summer look increasingly remote. But coach Cesare Maldini has tried most of the permutations available to him up front, and as his four goals for Chelsea against Barnsley in 1997 showed, Vialli only needs one chance to shine.

66 **I will be supporting Brazil.** 99
— *Gianluca Vialli before the 1994 World Cup Final*

DID YOU KNOW?
Vialli scored 11 goals in 20 games at under-21 level.

THIS PAGE: GIANLUCA VIALLI — ONE OF THE MOST INTELLIGENT FRONT-RUNNERS IN THE GAME.

OPPOSITE PAGE: DESPITE HIS UNDOUBTED TALENTS, VIALLI HAS STRUGGLED TO MAKE CHELSEA'S FIRST TEAM.

ATTACK
USA
WYNALDA

The United States all-time top goalscorer is widely regarded as the best player the country has at present. His prolific strike rate has certainly made him the most readily noticeable. Wynalda is the man who always grabs the glory by getting onto the end of his teammates' hard work. This goes a long way towards explaining how he has achieved such a high level of adulation among United States soccer aficionados, and it's got to be said that scoring more than a goal for every three international appearances is pretty good going by any striker's standards.

Wynalda started his career in 1987 by representing San Diego State University, and by Italia 90 he had become a regular in the national team. His obvious class earned him a contract in Europe and he became the first United States citizen to make it in Germany's Bundesliga. Despite worries that a player with no experience of European football would struggle to make the same impression on that side of the Atlantic, Wynalda proved himself capable of playing at the top level as a very effective and reliable striker. On his return to his native California, he was assigned by the MLS (Major League Soccer) to San José Clash, where he became a favourite with the fans. He is now fast approaching his 100th cap for the USA and with over 30 goals already under his belt, and still only just 29, he looks more than capable of doubling Bruce Murray's previous record of 22 goals for the national team.

Wynalda's experience at both club and international levels is crucial to his team. He has played in the last two World Cups, and had already become the USA's round ball hero well before the occasion when his free-kick earned the hosts a draw against Switzerland in the 1994 World Cup. Since then he's been part of the team that got to the semi-finals of the Copa America in 1995. He continues to spearhead a national team that is always improving, both tactically and in the quality of the players at its disposal.

FULL NAME:
Eric Wynalda

BORN:
9.6.69

BIRTHPLACE:
Fullerton CA

HEIGHT:
1.87/6ft 2in

WEIGHT:
86kg/ 13st 8lbs

CLUBS:
San Francisco Bay Blackhawks, FC Saarbrücken, VfL Bochum, San Jose Clash

DEBUT:
1989

66 I'm not Superman. I can't be expected to work wonders when I'm not 100%. 99
— *Eric Wynalda*

DID YOU KNOW?
Wynalda scored nine goals in his first ten games in the Bundesliga.

THIS PAGE: ERIC WYNALDA — THE FIRST US CITIZEN TO MAKE IT IN THE GERMAN BUNDESLIGA CELEBRATES YET ANOTHER GOAL.

OPPOSITE PAGE: WYNALDA RIDES A DEFENDER'S CHALLENGE AS THE USA LOSE 1–0 TO BRAZIL IN THE 1995 COPA AMERICA.

Chile
ZAMORANO

Chile's most influential player in recent years continues to lead their frontline after a decade of ups and downs in European football. 'Bam Bam' maintained his predominance in the national side by scoring 12 goals in qualifying for France 98, one more than Marcelo Salas (see page 73). His haul included two vital goals in Santiago as Chile defeated Paraguay 2–1, and five in a 6–0 win over Venezuela, despite missing a penalty.

Zamorano was born in the suburbs of Santiago, but first played for Cobresal, a small desert mining town of some 20,000 people in the extreme north of the country. He was then transferred to Cobre Andino, where he became the second division's top scorer, but returned to Cobresal for a second spell at the first division club before leaving his homeland for Switzerland in 1988.

He quickly began to make a name for himself in Europe, scoring 34 League goals in two years for St Gallen, and 21 for Andalucian club Seville in his first two years in Spain. However, to the dismay of Seville, Zamorano really started to bang the goals away when he went to rivals Real Madrid. Despite some periods of poor form when he couldn't seem to score at all, he netted 80 League goals in four years in the Spanish capital before moving to Italy. There, he joined Nwankwo Kanu (see page 40) and Frenchman Youri Djorkaeff in one of the most fearsome attacks in club football.

When Inter president Massimo Moratti continued to invest heavily in the transfer market by signing Ronaldo (see page 71) last summer, there was speculation that Zamorano would be sold, if not immediately, then soon. The rumour was fuelled by the story of Ronaldo demanding Inter's number 9 shirt, but Zamorano stayed and the Brazilian later gave up his claim in what the Chilean described as a 'phenomenal gesture, especially coming from the best player in the world'. That was high praise for his new teammate, but there are many Chileans who think Zamorano is the best player in the world.

FULL NAME:
Ivan Zamorano

BORN:
18.1.67

BIRTHPLACE:
Colonia de Maipu

HEIGHT:
1.78m/5ft 10in

WEIGHT:
72kg/11st 5lbs

CLUBS:
Cobresal, Cobre Andino, St Gallen, Seville, Real Madrid, Inter Milan

DEBUT:
1987

> **"** I knew that whenever Zamorano took a long run up, he always kicked it to the keeper's left. **"**
> — *Schalke goalkeeper Jens Lehman after saving Zamorano's penalty in the 1997 UEFA Cup Final*

DID YOU KNOW?
Zamorano scored 28 Spanish League goals in 1994/95 alone, and was ever present in the Real Madrid team.

THIS PAGE: IVAN ZAMORANO — STILL THE STAR OF CHILEAN FOOTBALL.

OPPOSITE PAGE: ZAMORANO RIDES ANOTHER CHALLENGE FOR INTER MILAN.

Born in a footballing backwater on the island of Sardinia, Zola began his career in 1985, but it wasn't until Napoli, then UEFA champions, paid £200,000 for him in 1989 that he became a recognized figure in Italian football. Zola earned three caps at Napoli, and after a £5m move to Parma in 1994, he scored a goal for every £1m in the 1995 UEFA Cup to help his new club to glory over Juventus in the final, taking Roberto Baggio's place in the Italian team in the process. He then scored in three successive Euro 96 qualifiers as Italy reached the finals, but then missed the penalty against Germany that put Italy out in the group stage.

Immediately after the disappointment of Euro 96, Zola found himself playing on the wing for Parma after the club signed Enrico Chiesa from Sampdoria. But with over a hundred Serie A games for both Napoli and Parma, and a total of 81 League goals, Chelsea coach Ruud Gullit noted that 'there are few strikers around of his quality', and wasted no time in signing the Italian. Since moving to London, Zola has been keeping his compatriot Gianluca Vialli (see page 86) out of the Chelsea team.

Zola is fast and can turn defenders inside out with the slightest drop of the shoulder. 'It could be because of my size that I can balance so well', he admits, but it is his skill that really sets him apart. His Chelsea teammate Mark Hughes says of his regular strike partner, 'He's so good on the ball, it's untrue'. That much could be seen in the way he controlled a long pass against England at Wembley before unleashing an unstoppable shot that won the game and, at the time, looked like taking Italy to the World Cup as group winners. That wasn't to be, but having eventually qualified through the play-offs, Zola will hope for a better World Cup than he had at USA 94, when he played just 12 minutes as a substitute against Nigeria before being sent off.

FULL NAME:
Gianfranco Zola

BORN:
5.7.66

BIRTHPLACE:
Oliena

HEIGHT:
1.68m/5ft 6in

WEIGHT:
65kg/10st 3lbs

CLUBS:
Nuroese, Torres, Napoli, Parma, Chelsea

DEBUT:
1991

❝ *It's so hard to do what he does.* **❞**
— *club coach Ruud Gullit*

DID YOU KNOW?
Napoli fans knew him as 'Marazola', after Maradona, the former occupant of the club's number 10 shirt.

THIS PAGE: GIANFRANCO ZOLA — A PLAYER WHO HAS TURNED SIZE TO HIS ADVANTAGE.

OPPOSITE PAGE: HIS STRENGTH AND INCREDIBLE CLOSE CONTROL MAKE ZOLA VERY DIFFICULT TO SHAKE OFF THE BALL.

NAME:
Ferenc Puskas

COUNTRY:
Hungary

WORLD CUPS:
1954, 1958, 1962 (for Spain)
His dynamite left-foot was legendary,
first for Hungary and then in his
adopted country Spain.

NAME:
Manoel Francisco dos Santos
'Garrincha'

COUNTRY:
Brazil

WORLD CUPS:
1958, 1962, 1966
Garrincha was the paciest and most
skilful right-winger Brazil ever had.
He was as important to the team as
Pelé himself.

NAME:
Sir Robert 'Bobby' Charlton

COUNTRY:
England

WORLD CUPS:
1966, 1970
Bobby Charlton's surging runs from
his deep-lying centre-forward role
made him England's most famous
player ever.

NAME:
Jair Ventura Filho 'Jairzinho'

COUNTRY:
Brazil

WORLD CUPS:
1966, 1970
The successor to Garrincha played
alongside his hero at England 66
before creating a new record by
scoring in every round in Mexico 70.

NAME:
Michel Platini

COUNTRY:
France

WORLD CUPS:
1978, 1982
A great ball player who promised
much in 1978 and then inspired
France to within an inch of the
1982 final.

TACTICAL INNOVATIONS

THE FIRST MIDFIELDER
4–3–3
Hungary's answer to the 'stopper'
introduced shortly before the first
World Cup was to drop their centre-
forward in deep where he could avoid
getting clobbered throughout the
match. It was from this position that
Ferenc Puskas controlled his near-
invincible team, and the concept of
the midfield as a zone on the pitch
distinct from defence and attack
began with him. In France 98 the
home side may well prove themselves
masters of it this time round.

THE GREATEST

NAME:
Johan Cruyff

COUNTRY:
Holland

BORN: 25.4.47

BIRTHPLACE:
Amsterdam

WORLD CUPS:
1974

CAPS:
48 (33 goals)

MOMENT OF GLORY

With their inspirational captain playing at the hub of a team of so many highly talented stars, Holland were everyone's favourites to win in 1974. Cruyff's tremendous skill and athleticism were combined with the unusual understanding of the game he had learned over the many years since he first represented Ajax at the age of 12. From his central position as an attacking midfielder, he would appear anywhere on the pitch, often with the ball at his feet. Cruyff, like Beckenbauer (see page 169), later took his leadership qualities into management despite lacking official qualifications. He enjoyed immense success at club level with both Ajax and Barcelona.

Although Cruyff had retired from international football by 1978 and so was not part of the Dutch side that reached the final in Argentina, he was its greatest star in 1974, possibly the greatest all-rounder of all time, and the epitome of 'Total Football'. His son Jordi, who learned his football under his father's tutelage at Barcelona before his move to Manchester United, should feature in the Dutch squad for France 98. There, Cruyff Jr will choose to wear his first name on his shirt to avoid any comparison with his legendary father.

Attacker moves back to midfield

Mexico
GARCIA ASPE

Garcia Aspe first caught the eye in 1984 when he was voted Best Young Player of the Year in Mexico. Less than a year later, he was selected to play for the Mexican national youth team against the USSR and made his full international debut in a 4–1 victory over Honduras in 1988. He was part of the team that got to the final of the Copa America in Ecuador in 1993 and was also in the squad that reached the World Cup Finals in the USA the following year. His contribution to Mexican football was eventually recognized when he was voted 1997 Mexican Player of the Year.

But things haven't been going too well for the national team recently. Some questionable performances against supposedly inferior opposition in qualifying led to some poor results, not least of which was a disappointing 0–0 draw against the United States where Garcia Aspe played as one half of a two-man midfield. That formation made the team look distinctly weak in the middle of the park, as both he and Galindo, his midfield partner that day, are very much ball players rather than ball winners. And although Mexico eventually qualified with ease, Serbian-born coach Bora Milutinovic has come under a lot of criticism in his adopted country for his employment of strategies such as this 5–2–3 formation, and many people called for him to be replaced before the team left for France. But such criticisms have not been made on the basis of his selecting the country's most influential midfielder of the past decade and one of their better performers at USA 94, where he played two games and scored one goal.

Given that Mexico had qualified, after they failed to reach Italia 90, Milutinovic was expected to remain as coach at least until after the World Cup. But the Serb was sensationally sacked after the team had claimed their place at France 98, and the Mexicans will finalize their preparations without him.

Garcia Aspe, of course, remains.

FULL NAME:
Alberto Garcia Aspe

BORN:
11.5.67

BIRTHPLACE:
Mexico City

HEIGHT:
1.71m/5ft 7in

WEIGHT:
71kg/11st 3lbs

CLUBS:
UNAM, Necaxa, River Plate, America, Necaxa

DEBUT:
1988

66 **This is sport, and everything should be decided on the pitch.** 99
— *Alberto Garcia Aspe*

DID YOU KNOW?
Garcia Aspe has been sent off three times for his country.

THIS PAGE: GARCIA ASPE — ONE PLAYER WHO CAN TRANSFORM PERENNIAL UNDER-ACHIEVERS MEXICO INTO WORLD BEATERS.

OPPOSITE PAGE: THE MIDFIELDER'S WORLD CUP EXPERIENCE IS INDISPENSIBLE TO HIS TEAM.

Morocco
AZZOUZI

FULL NAME:
Rachid Azzouzi

BORN:
10.11.71

BIRTHPLACE:
Casablanca

HEIGHT:
1.81m/6ft

WEIGHT:
76kg/12st

CLUBS:
MSV Duisburg, Fortuna Köln,
Greuther Fuerth

There is still a lingering impression of African football teams being rather disorganized and over-optimistic in attack and too naive in defence to really compete for the World Cup; but the way in which both Morocco and Tunisia chase opponents down in midfield makes a mockery of this stereotype. Both teams have employed experienced foreign coaches who believe that the best form of defence is attack. So players who are prepared to compete for the ball in the opposition half and not allow their defences to be exposed to prolonged pressure are currently enjoying a boom time in North African football. Rachid Azzouzi is a case in point. Sitting in the middle of the park for Morocco, he is a player who won't let the opposition dwell on the ball, and his skill and passing abilities make him an important possession player for the team as well.

The long-haired powerhouse was part of the Moroccan team at USA 94, but even his hard running in the heat of the American summer was not enough for Morocco as the team went straight back home after three successive defeats. But they qualified easily this time and look a far more impressive side. Rachid Azzouzi has had the opportunity to play in one of the toughest leagues in the world in Germany and has become a highly experienced player at international level.

He joined Greuther Fuerth in the second division of the German Bundesliga a year ago, and although he may now have taken a step down in his club football, Azzouzi is still very much part of coach Henri Michel's plans for the World Cup in France. His experience at USA 94 will be vital if the team is to live up to the high expectations at home. And with Azzouzi still battling for the ball in midfield, you can expect Morocco to do rather better in France, where they will undoubtedly be very well supported by expatriates living in the country, as well as by people travelling north from Spain and Morocco.

> 66 **With Azzouzi still battling for the ball in midfield, you can expect Morocco to do rather better in France.** 99

DID YOU KNOW?
Azzouzi scored the last goal of the 1994/95 season for Duisburg before moving to Köln.

THIS PAGE: RACHID AZZOUZI — INTEGRAL TO MOROCCO'S STYLE OF PLAY.

OPPOSITE PAGE: RACHID AZZOUZI HOLDS OFF THE CHALLENGE OF SAUDI ARABIA'S SAMI AL-JABER AT USA 94.

Ba is a rising star with bleached blond hair who likes to wear the normally unfavoured number 13 shirt. Although he has yet to stake his claim to a regular first-team place, this young talent may well come to prominence in France 98. If his fledgling international career is allowed to continue to develop, he will torment left-backs at France 98 with his tremendous power, energy, athleticism and dribbling prowess. He is fast, has good control, the ability to surprise and has demonstrated his cool finishing on the night of his international debut.

His father was himself a left-back for Le Havre who, fortunately for France, nurtured a love of the game in his son. Now it looks like all those early football lessons will reap huge dividends.

Having been let go by Paris St Germain as a teenager, 'Ibou' made his name at his father's old club. He played five seasons for Le Havre before moving to Bordeaux, where he felt he had a better chance of winning honours. Then, after turning in half a season of excellent performances at a high profile club, he was selected for the friendly against Portugal. He took his chance well, setting up Didier Deschamps's (see page 120) goal and capping that with his own.

On the downside, he is known to get lost out on the wing and fade out of games occasionally. However, as he accumulates international experience he will gain the confidence to know that he can come looking for the ball, and get it, even when things aren't going well. That in turn will encourage him to get forward more to make and score the goals his team so desperately need. The French will hope their distinctive winger becomes as consistent for his country as he was for their clubs.

FULL NAME:
Ibrahim Ba

BORN:
12.11.73

BIRTHPLACE:
Dakar, Senegal

HEIGHT:
1.80m/5ft 11in

WEIGHT:
70kg/11st 4lbs

CLUBS:
Abbeville, Paris St Germain, Paris FC, Chantilly, Le Havre, Bordeaux, AC Milan

DEBUT:
1997

66 **Every time he gets the ball, you have the feeling he is going to make something happen.** 99
— *ex-Bordeaux teammate Laurent Croci*

DID YOU KNOW?
The bleached hair is an imitation of his favourite basketball star, the American Dennis Rodman.

THIS PAGE: IBRAHIM BA — FRANCE'S NEW SENEGALESE WING SENSATION IS SET TO MAKE HIS WORLD CUP DEBUT IN HIS ADOPTED COUNTRY.

OPPOSITE PAGE: IN ACTION AGAINST HOLLAND AT THE START OF HIS INTERNATIONAL CAREER.

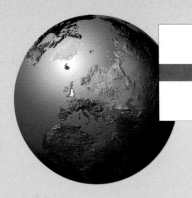

MIDFIELD
England
BECKHAM

FULL NAME:
David Robert Beckham

BORN:
2.5.75

BIRTHPLACE:
Leytonstone

HEIGHT:
1.78m/5ft 10in

WEIGHT:
71kg/11st 2lbs

CLUBS:
Manchester United

DEBUT:
1996

Manchester United's midfield sensation has become an established regular in the England set-up since Euro 96. He first burst onto the public consciousness with an amazing strike against Wimbledon from just inside his own half on the opening day of the 1996/97 season. He had been at Old Trafford since he was 16 and became part of the 1995/96 first team squad following the sale of Andrei Kanchelskis, but that lob over Wimbledon's Scottish international, Neil Sullivan, at Selhurst Park lifted expectations of him to an altogether higher level. He has quickly proved himself capable of living up to those expectations.

Making his England debut a month later, he immediately settled into international football and in two seasons has gradually become a fixture in the team. Although his marking can be a little suspect, he is a very complete ball player who tackles resolutely and shoots well. He is also a dead-ball expert with a run up that consists of a quick skip and a slightly unorthodox side-footed strike at the ball. He is as accurate as anyone on the team in that situation and will take most of England's corners and many of their free-kicks.

He has already won both the Premiership and the FA Cup with Manchester United and scored on his European debut against Galatasaray. For a while it seemed his international place would have to wait until Gascoigne's departure, but the England midfield has since shown that it can accommodate both players. In qualification, Beckham was employed at right wing-back, where his pace and willingness to take players on poses a constant threat to defences. But he usually looks best when allowed to drift in field and spray his long, sweeping passes around the pitch. If Coach Glenn Hoddle feels confident in leaving the midfield holding duties to Paul Ince (see page 132), he is likely to play Beckham alongside Paul Gascoigne (see page 127) in the middle. While the sight of this young Londoner standing over a free-kick will be unfamiliar to most of the world, if he is anywhere within sight of goal, it will raise English expectations further than ever.

66 He has responded well to international football and shown that he is capable of playing at this level. **99**
— *England coach Glenn Hoddle*

DID YOU KNOW?
Beckham won the FA Youth Cup in his first season at Old Trafford.

THIS PAGE: DAVID BECKHAM — SET TO MAKE HIS MARK IN INTERNATIONAL FOOTBALL.

OPPOSITE PAGE: IN ACTION FOR ENGLAND IN THE DEFEAT OF GEORGIA IN QUALIFYING.

SUPERSTARS OF THE WORLD CUP

Tunisia
BEYA

The 1995 and 1996 Tunisian Player of the Year is the national team's midfield creator and the focus of much of their possession football. Cut him out of the game, and the likes of Mehdi Ben Slimane and Adel Sellimi don't get the service they require. It is Beya's close control and vision that allow him to calmly direct operations from the centre-circle with accurate passes that bring out the best in his teammates, while those around him maintain the high midfield work-rate that is the trademark of Tunisian football.

'Zouba' has been playing his club football in the ancient coastal town of Sousse since 1991. Although there has again recently been talk of him going to show off his skills in the German Bundesliga, it looks like he will be playing in the red-and-white of Etoile for the foreseeable future. After making his international debut in 1994, Beya could probably have gone to make his fame and fortune in Europe, but chose to stay in his homeland to guide Etoile to the Pan-African Cup in 1995 and the Tunisian Cup the following year. The team then went on to win their seventh domestic Cup in 1996 and their seventh Tunisian League title in 1997, again reaching the final of the Pan-African Club Cup in both seasons.

Despite goals from their star player in recent victories over Egypt, Senegal, Olympique Marseille and Zambia, the Tunisians are likely to struggle in France. 1–0 home defeats to Japan and Australia in the qualifiers said a lot for the great strides those two nations have made in recent years, but neither could be considered a world force. The Tunisians are going to need their most influential playmaker to be at the very top of his form if they are going to make any sort of impression in France. Beya and company will be playing not only for the World Cup, but also for the memory of defender Hedi Ben Rekhissa, who died recently after collapsing during a friendly match for Tunisian club side Esperance.

FULL NAME:
Zoubeir Beya

BORN:
15.5.71

BIRTHPLACE:
Msaken

HEIGHT:
1.86m/6ft 1in

WEIGHT:
78kg/12st 4lbs

CLUBS:
Msaken, Esperance, Etoile Sportive de Sahel

DEBUT:
1994

> 66 **Zoubeir Beya is a class act.** 99
> — *South African football press*

DID YOU KNOW?
Beya scored his country's only goal in a recent 3–1 defeat by neighbours Morocco.

THIS PAGE: ZUBEIR BEYA — TUNISIA'S STAR AND MOST INFLUENTIAL PLAYER.

OPPOSITE PAGE: ZOUBA PLAYS CENTRALLY, BUT LIKES TO MOVE OUT TOWARDS THE LEFT AS HE COMES FORWARD.

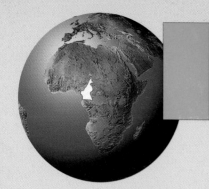

Cameroon
BIYICK

FULL NAME:
Francois Omam Biyick

BORN:
21.05.66

BIRTHPLACE:
Sack Bayerne

HEIGHT:
1.83m/6ft

WEIGHT:
80kg/12st 8lbs

CLUBS:
Canon Yaounde, Laval, Rennes, Cannes, Marseille, Lens, FC America

DEBUT:
1985

INTERNATIONAL HONOURS:
African Nations Cup winner 1988

66 **Marco van Basten played in my centre-forward position as I wish I could play.** 99
— *Francois Omam Biyick*

DID YOU KNOW?
As an unknown who scarcely qualified as a professional, Biyick cost French club Laval £75,000.

THIS PAGE: FRANCOIS OMAM BIYICK — A VETERAN CAMPAIGNER WITH A WEALTH OF WORLD CUP EXPERIENCE.

OPPOSITE PAGE: WINNING THE BALL IN MIDFIELD.

The man who scored the first goal of the 1990 World Cup is back in the Cameroon team. In that famous match against World Cup holders Argentina on the first day of Italia 90, Biyick completed the move that sunk the champions and announced the arrival of the 'Lions of Africa' as serious competitors in world football.

Early in the game, Cyrille Makanaky played a tempting cross from the left. Biyick rose to beat Roberto Sensini (see page 222) to the ball and headed past keeper Nery Pumpido. Until that moment, Omam Biyick says he was 'a nobody – just another footballer'. That goal made him a star and wrote his name in the history books. It was the shock of the tournament at the time, but Cameroon 1 Argentina 0 no longer looks like a freak result.

Of course, that goal in 1990 isn't this player's sole contribution to his country's efforts. Francois Omam Biyick has all the qualities of a traditional centre-forward. He is strong, hard-running and alert. He has height, and he uses it well, as Argentina already well know. He shows good movement off the ball, using his experience to guess where it is most likely break out for the chance of a shot on goal. And he is also very good at holding play up, a skill that does not diminish with age but does improve with experience.

In the USA 94 qualifiers, he scored the opener against Zimbabwe in the final qualifying match, earning his right to play in World Cup finals for a second time. Out of favour for a while since then, when it was thought that his international career might have come to an end, he has recently been recalled to the team. Not only is he one of the team's most likely sources of a goal, he also drops back into midfield for extended periods to help his teammates develop the passing moves that give confidence to any side. An international career that spans 13 years would be well concluded with an improvement on Cameroon's 1990 quarter-final berth.

Croatia
BOBAN

Zvonimir Boban is the captain and brains of this highly regarded Croatian team. Very much an attacking player who likes to sit in the centre of midfield and concentrate on what is going on in front of him rather than behind him, he has great technique, especially when running with the ball, and is a constant source of goalscoring opportunities.

As a youngster with Dinamo Zagreb in 1985, Boban stood out in a team of stars as a very exciting prospect for the future. Although the records show that he didn't make his debut in the newly-formed Croatian national team until he was 22, he had previously played for Yugoslavia. When he took part in a 2–0 defeat of Romania on Christmas Eve 1990, he had by then collected eight caps for Yugoslavia before the break up of that state, and had been part of Yugoslavia's victorious U-18 World Championship winning side in 1987. He left Croatia for Italy in 1992 and first played for Bari in the south east of the country before reaching the pinnacle of his club career by signing for AC Milan in 1992. He was later to team up with compatriot Robert Prosinecki (see page 154) at the mighty Milan club. He has won three Italian Championships and the European Super Cup with AC Milan.

Europe did not see the best of Boban at Euro 96. He was injured in the build-up to the finals and was not fully match fit. However, he still made an enormous contribution to the 3–1 defeat of Denmark that brought his third international goal after receiving a pass from Davor Suker (see page 85).

But even when he is fully fit, Boban is not a player who will run hard for the full 90 minutes. He is a great asset to the team, but his class shows in the final third of the pitch, where his imagination and creativity can produce goalscoring chances out of nowhere. And with the world class forward line he has playing in front of him, Zvonimir Boban is a lot of people's favourite to lift the World Cup in July.

FULL NAME:	
Zvonimir Boban	
BORN:	
8.10.68	
BIRTHPLACE:	
Imotski	
HEIGHT:	
1.84m/6ft	
WEIGHT:	
78kg/12st 4lbs	
CLUBS:	
Dinamo Zagreb (now FC Croatia), Bari, AC Milan	
DEBUT:	
1990	

" Just like all my colleagues, I am extremely honoured to pull on the red and white shirt of Croatia. **"**
— *Boban*

DID YOU KNOW?
Boban became captain of Dinamo Zagreb when he was still only 18.

THIS PAGE: ZVONIMIR BOBAN — SENSATIONAL IN ATTACK, HE IS OFTEN CRITICIZED FOR NEGLECTING HIS DEFENSIVE DUTIES.

OPPOSITE PAGE: WORLD CUP DEBUTANTS CROATIA WILL DEPEND UPON THEIR MIDFIELD SCHEMER FOR GOALSCORING OPPORTUNITIES.

Holland
COCU

This nippy attacking midfield player gives the Dutch team a lot of attacking options. The Dutch are not over-blessed with pace in midfield and attack, and that can restrict them when they're trying to push forward. Cocu's tireless running is a good counter-point to the laid-back skills of the flair players on the side.

He was, by Dutch standards, a late starter in international football who didn't play for his country until the build up to Euro 96, when he was already 25. This meant that, unlike so many of his more illustrious teammates, he was a virtual unknown outside his own country until he played in the quarter-final against France. It was to be no glorious entrance, however. Holland lost that game on penalties, but Cocu's impressive contribution to the team effort was there for all to see and he has since settled into becoming a regular for the Dutch national team.

Although he was initially selected as a temporary replacement for Clarence Seedorf (see page 159) when the Surinamese player's form took a nose-dive, he has now done well enough in the team for coach Guus Hiddink to consider playing him on the left alongside the Real Madrid player.

Cocu is Holland's busybody in midfield. A player who prefers to play in a slightly more advanced position than Seedorf, he has the knack of eluding his marker and slipping into the danger area, where he is quick and deadly. He has scored some important goals and shows an eye for getting into the right place at the right time, as when he got a touch to cross from Dennis Bergkamp (see page 25) in the 7–1 demolition of Wales in qualifying for France. The clinical finishing he showed against Eire is a reminder that the PSV star is an accomplished professional who has been around the block in Holland and has the valuable experience of some competitive international action under his belt from Euro 96.

FULL NAME:
Phillip Cocu

BORN:
29.10.70

BIRTHPLACE:
Eindhoven

HEIGHT:
1.75m/5ft 9in

WEIGHT:
80kg/12st 8lbs

CLUBS:
Zevenaar, De Graafschap, AFC '34 Alkmaar, AZ Alkmaar, Vitesse Arnhem, PSV Eindhoven

DEBUT:
1996

> 66 He is, of course, an important player. 99
> — *club coach Dick Advocaat*

DID YOU KNOW?
Cocu won the Dutch Cup with PSV Eindhoven in 1996.

THIS PAGE: COCU CHASES AFTER THE BALL IN THE 7–1 THRASHING OF WALES IN QUALIFYING.

OPPOSITE PAGE: CONTRIBUTING TO HOLLAND'S 7–1 ANNIHILATION OF WALES IN QUALIFYING, NOVEMBER 9TH, 1996.

Scotland
COLLINS

FULL NAME:
John Collins

BORN:
31.1.68

BIRTHPLACE:
Galashiels

HEIGHT:
1.75m/5ft 9in

WEIGHT:
74kg/11st 9lbs

CLUBS:
Hibernian, Glasgow Celtic, Monaco

DEBUT:
1988

This left-sided midfielder with the delicate left foot has earned a reputation over the last decade as one of the most skilful players in Scottish football. So much so that when he signed for Celtic in 1990, the Glasgow club paid out a record £1m for his services. Coach Billy McNeill made two other high profile signings that summer, bringing Arsenal reserve Martin Hayes to the club as well as the wayward genius of Charlie Nicholas from Aberdeen. Neither of these latter two were to make much of an impression in Glasgow, but over the next six years, the little left winger proved himself worth every penny of his transfer fee.

John Collins scored some crucial goals in his time at Celtic, including a wonderfully flighted free-kick against arch-rivals Rangers in a 2–0 win at Ibrox in 1994, the penalty against Kilmarnock that put Celtic into the semi-finals of the 1995 Scottish Cup where they were to overcome his former club before going on to win the trophy, and the penalty that resulted in the first ever goal in front of Celtic Park's new North Stand.

Collins moved to Monaco in the summer of 1996 and immediately started keeping the talented Nigerian international Viktor Ikpeba out of the first eleven. His presence lifted the principality's team to fresh glory, winning the French League in his first season with them by a convincing 12 points over closest rivals PSG. As befits his services to the team, Monaco's Scottish import has now been elevated to the club captaincy.

He is used to best effect when attacking defences from the left side of midfield. With the ball at his feet he will either cut inside to penetrate the penalty area himself, or, more often, he will head for the by-line from where he consistently delivers dangerous crosses for his strikers. His ability at free-kicks also gives the Scots extra options whenever he stands over the ball with his captain Gary McAllister (see page 142), and he has also proved himself to be a clinical penalty taker whose services in that department may well be called upon in the course of France 98.

66 **I don't normally run 70 yards with the ball, never mind go round the keeper and score.** 99
— *John Collins after scoring against San Marino in 1995*

DID YOU KNOW?
When Collins helped Monaco win the French League in 1997, it was their first title since 1988.

THIS PAGE: JOHN COLLINS — HIS EXPERIENCE IN FRENCH FOOTBALL SHOULD BE TO SCOTLAND'S ADVANTAGE AT THE WORLD CUP.

OPPOSITE PAGE: SCOTLAND'S CLASSY MIDFIELDER IN ACTION AGAINST FELLOW QUALIFIERS AUSTRIA.

Belgium
DE BILDE

The bad boy of Belgian football is rebuilding his career in Holland after being the aggressor in one of the most disturbing on-pitch incidents in recent world football history. Playing for Anderlecht against his previous club Aalst, the highly skilful attacking midfielder became fed up with the tight marking of Krist Porte. In a momentary fit of rage he hit his opponent in the face so hard that he broke Porte's nose, eye socket and bruised his retina. The referee was looking the other way and saw nothing, but the police saw it all and promptly arrested and charged de Bilde. He was banned from football for three months.

Unable to play in his own country, de Bilde then signed for PSV Eindhoven in Holland through a loophole in his ban restriction. The Dutch Federation ruled that if he signed for the club before March 7th, he could play in Holland that spring, and FIFA went along with their ruling. De Bilde, despite his deep regret over the incident, is a professional footballer and was keen to further his career, so he accepted the get-out clause that the world governing body had left him. He went north and promptly scored seven goals for PSV before the end of the season, guiding his new club to the Dutch league title.

League rivals Feyenoord had been keen to sign the player too, but they were less persevering in their attempts to persuade FIFA to allow him to return to the game. It is widely held in Holland that the league was decided off the pitch that year. Jim Calderwood, coach of Willem II, put it succinctly: 'If Feyenoord had got de Bilde, they would have been champions and not PSV.'

De Bilde is now back in the Belgian squad, where his exciting footballing skills will be more than welcome in France, and the spectacle of the World Cup will surely benefit from his presence. But it makes you wonder what Feyenoord, Aalst and, of course, poor Krist Porte, will make of the way he was let off the hook.

FULL NAME:
Gilles de Bilde

BORN:
9.6.71

BIRTHPLACE:
Zellik

HEIGHT:
1.83m/6ft

WEIGHT:
78kg/12st 4lbs

CLUBS:
Zellik, HO Merchtem, Eendracht, Aalst, Anderlecht, PSV Eindhoven

DEBUT:
1994

> **❝ I am very grateful to PSV for giving me the chance to show there is more to me than some of the headlines have suggested. ❞**
> — *Gilles de Bilde*

DID YOU KNOW?
De Bilde was voted Belgian Player of the Year in 1994.

THIS PAGE: GILLES DE BILDE — ALWAYS AN AGGRESSIVE PLAYER, HE IS OUT TO PROVE THAT HE HAS LEFT HIS MOST INFAMOUS INCIDENT BEHIND HIM.

OPPOSITE PAGE: A STRONG TACKLER WHO IS BECOMING AN ACCOMPLISHED ATTACKER.

Holland
DE BOER

In 1996, Ronald de Boer became the Dutch players' Player of the Year for the third time in his illustrious career. The player who now sits in behind Dennis Bergkamp (see page 25) in the national team started out his career as a prolific striker in the youth teams. But it wasn't long before his club decided that his great ball skills should put to more frequent use in the middle of the park. However, if Holland suffer any injuries up front, Ronald de Boer is likely to play there. He is an accomplished goalscorer and the Dutch have an abundance of skilful midfielders sitting on the bench waiting to take over as the right-sided playmaker of the team.

Although both Ronald and his twin Frank are very much in the Ajax mould, both show a lot of mobility on the pitch and are blessed with consummate skills – neither of the de Boer brothers is entirely Ajax. The Ajax net failed to catch them as young boys and they first played together for a local side before they signed for Holland's most prestigious club. Ajax weren't too far behind, though. The boys were only 13 when they left the De Zouaven youth team in nearby Lutjebroek. They then began to travel up to Amsterdam with former Ajax youth trainer Louis van Gaal, who also lived in Hoorn at the time, and was only too pleased to give them a lift.

But while his brother has spent all the rest of his career at Ajax, Ronald de Boer moved to FC Twente Enschede in 1991. Although he was successful there, this wasn't to be a long separation from the club that nurtured him. Van Gaal signed him back to Ajax at the beginning of 1993. His contract, like that of his twin, was due to run out directly after France 98, but has now been extended for another six years. Ajax win things. Ronald de Boer and his brother have won the Dutch Cup, the League Championship, the Dutch Super Cup, the UEFA Cup, the European Cup, as well as the European and World Super Cups. Just the World Cup to go then.

FULL NAME:
Ronald de Boer

BORN:
15.5.70

BIRTHPLACE:
Hoorn

HEIGHT:
1.81m/5ft 11in

WEIGHT:
77kg/12st 2lbs

CLUBS:
FC Twente, Ajax

DEBUT:
1990

> **The essential thing to being a good footballer is that you play as part of the team.**
> — *Ronald de Boer*

DID YOU KNOW?
Ronald de Boer also made his Ajax debut against PEC Zwolle. Ajax won 6–4 on November 22nd, 1987.

THIS PAGE: RONALD DE BOER – THE RIGHT-SIDED MIDFIELDER IS A FIXTURE IN THE DUTCH TEAM.

OPPOSITE PAGE: AN ALL-ROUND FOOTBALLER VERY MUCH IN THE AJAX MOULD.

Brazil
DENILSON

FULL NAME:
Denilson de Oliveira

BORN:
24.8.77

BIRTHPLACE:
São Bernado do Campo, São Paolo

HEIGHT:
1.72m/5ft 8in

WEIGHT:
62kg/9st 9lbs

CLUBS:
São Bernado do Campo,
São Paolo, Real Betis

DEBUT
1997

HONOURS
Copa America winner 1997

**“ All my coaches have
encouraged me
to dribble. ”**
— Denilson

DID YOU KNOW?
If Denilson stays at Betis for the
duration of his contract, he will
eventually cost them some £250m.

THIS PAGE: DENILSON – THE WORLD'S MOST
EXPENSIVE PLAYER WILL BE LOOKING TO
JUSTIFY HIS £20M PRICE TAG.

OPPOSITE PAGE: BRINGING THE BALL UNDER
CONTROL AGAINST ITALY AT EURO 96.

Like so many Brazilian players, Denilson comes from a very poor background. He was born in the rural São Paolo hinterland where, he says, many of his childhood friends 'followed the wrong paths in life'. Some 'disappeared', others just died. He believes he could well have suffered the same fate, if it hadn't been for football.

A São Paolo player since 1989, he was first seen by coach Banha playing for his home town of São Bernado do Campo. At 15, he was invited by coach Tele Santana to join the professional staff. He considers himself lucky to have scored against Sporting Cristal in his first full game in the 1994 Conmebol: 'Many good players don't make it for a lack of chances. I made it in my first game.'

He reached the national under-19 team at the age of 17. Although his selfish style prevented him from becoming a regular at that time, when he was eventually selected to play left-side midfield for the national team, he wreaked havoc with the Cameroon and Bosnian defences in two successive man-of-the-match performances. Since then, he has been keeping Juninho (see page 136) out of the team and is also being tipped as Leonardo's natural successor. In Andalucia, he is already on the pennants of many bars, though he has yet to kick a ball for Betis.

This is because although he signed for the Seville club last summer for a world-record fee in excess of £20m, he will not start his 11-year contract until after France 98. Betis obviously believe they have a bargain, as his value will have risen considerably by then, even at that price.

However, he needs to improve his marksmanship; even when he was playing up front for Palmeiras, there were midfielders scoring more goals than him. But there will be few players at France 98 who can match him for pure skill.

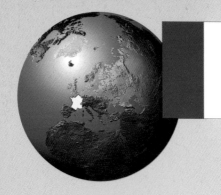

FULL NAME:
Didier Deschamps

BORN:
15.10.68

BIRTHPLACE:
Bayonne

HEIGHT:
1.74m/5ft 9in

WEIGHT:
71kg/11st 3lbs

CLUBS:
Bayonne, Nantes, Marseille,
Bordeaux, Juventus

DEBUT:
1989

For all the exciting talent the French will have on display, it is the Juventus midfield anchorman who is still very much the number one star of French football. When Eric Cantona said that Deschamps was a 'porteur d'eau' (water-carrier), it was the prodigiously talented 'Erique' who was dropped from the side. That's how highly the French football establishment rates Deschamps.

He has a great talent for the telling pass but is sometimes criticized for not using his skill to attacking affect. However, the holding role suits him. He has never been noted as a goalscorer – he's averaged just over a goal per season in his 13-year career – he remains very much at the heart of the French midfield along with his club and international colleague Zinedine Zidane (see page 166).

Although he suggests that 'perhaps I'll be told to play a little further up from time to time', the fact that he plays in a deeper position for Juve than he does for France seems to be working for his whole game. His form is undoubtedly improving with the responsibilities of the more defensive anchor role he assumed after Paolo Sousa left Juve for Borussia Dortmund.

Deschamps's contribution to the team's performance may not be eye-catching, but if France are to succeed on their own soil, Deschamps will be silent architect behind it, snuffing out opponents' attacks and turning the play to his own team's advantage.

66 **He and I understand each other's game perfectly.** 99
— *Zinedine Zidane*

DID YOU KNOW?
Didier Deschamps has won the European Cup with two different clubs: Marseille in 1993 and Juventus in 1996.

THIS PAGE: DIDIER DESCHAMPS — A SOLID AND EXPERIENCED PLAYER WHO NEVER SHIRKS HIS TEAM RESPONSIBILITIES.

OPPOSITE PAGE: KEEPING UP THE PRESSURE AGAINST PORTUGAL IN JANUARY 1996.

Brazil
DJALMINHA

A newcomer to the squad, his extraordinary talent and visionary passes can transform a move and leave defences completely wrong-footed. Though vastly experienced, and very much the brains of the Palmeiras side that won 32 of 35 matches to take the São Paolo Championship, he only made his international debut after he had proved himself there. Playing to the best of his ability he can stand out as Brazil's finest exponent of *o jogo bonito* (the beautiful game).

He was kicked out of Flamengo in 1993 after fighting with teammate Renato Portaluppi. He has since been accused of arrogance in the Brazilian press, though much of the reason he hasn't been selected before now can be put down to his fiery temperament. He signed for Guarani after this incident, but it wasn't until he went to Japan that he got real first-team experience.

His temperament now seemingly controlled, he currently plays for Deportivo in Spain, for whom he signed at the same time as his Palmeiras teammate Luizao. Though he played up front with Luizao for Palmeiras, his preferred position is much deeper. From here he has more options, including Bebeto, a winner at USA 94 and also hoping for a place in the squad at France 98. The two together can be quite devastating, though it will cost any club in excess of £60m to take Djalminha away from La Coruña.

The left-footed player who never looks like he's in a hurry will remember that his father, Djalma Dias (who won 16 caps, five more than his son had at the time of going to press) was the big surprise omission from the victorious 1970 World Cup squad. His son, who has just completed his first ever season in Europe, knows that he is playing for his place.

FULL NAME:
Djalma Feitosa Dias

BORN:
09.12.70

BIRTHPLACE:
São Paolo

HEIGHT:
1.76m/5ft 8in

WEIGHT:
68kg/10st 10lbs

CLUBS:
Vasco da Gama, Flamengo, Guarani, Shimizu, Palmeiras, Deportivo de la Coruña

DEBUT
1996

HONOURS:
Copa America winner 1997

❝ I know that in modern football speed and power have become more important, but the emphasis in my game is always on skill and technique. ❞
— *Djalminha*

DID YOU KNOW?
The often harsh Brazilian press elected him their Player of the Year in 1996.

THIS PAGE: DJALMINHA — EVEN IN BRAZIL, THE DEPORTIVO PLAYER IS NOTED FOR HIS BALL SKILL.

OPPOSITE PAGE: STRETCHING TO PROTECT THE BALL FROM THE HOSTS AT LE TOURNOI.

MIDFIELD
Jamaica
EARLE

J amaica's highest profile player is a powerful footballer who wins a lot of balls in midfield and loves to get forward into attack. Since moving to Wimbledon, he has consistently been one of their best players and has scored more than enough goals to make him an outside candidate for the England team. But the chance to play for his homeland never came, and at the age of 30, Robbie Earle decided to cast his lot in with Jamaica, a team on the verge of its first ever World Cup appearance. Since then, he has travelled regularly to the Caribbean to join the squad in the final stages of qualification and preparation for France.

Robbie Earle made his English league debut in 1982 after coming up through the ranks of his local youth team. He had become a regular for Vale by 1984 and helped them climb from the old Fourth Division to the Second by the 1988/89 season. His contribution was noted higher up the League and in the summer of 1991, Wimbledon paid out £775,000 to take him to the top flight.

His crunching tackles and well-timed runs from deep made him an immediate success in London and he played 40 games in his first season, finishing up as the Dons' second top scorer with 14 goals. He was the only ever-present player in the team the following year and looked well on his way to the England squad. But then he missed the start of the 1994/95 season through injury. He returned to the Wimbledon team before Christmas but was out again three months later for the rest of the season. That misfortune probably cost him his England place.

There are a lot of excellent homegrown players in the English Premiership who have cast their international lot in with other countries. Robbie Earle's club colleague Vinnie Jones has elected to represent Wales instead of England. But while Jones will miss the World Cup this summer, Robbie Earle is going to France with the Reggae Boyz.

FULL NAME:
Robbie Earle

BORN:
27.1.65

BIRTHPLACE:
Newcastle-under-Lyme, England

HEIGHT:
1.78m/5ft 10in

WEIGHT:
68kg/10st 10lbs

CLUBS:
Port Vale, Wimbledon

DEBUT:
1997

66 **In Jamaica's case, it's more than a matter of football, it's about discovering a national identity.** 99
— *Robbie Earle*

DID YOU KNOW?
Robbie Earle was pencilled into the England squad for Le Tournoi.

THIS PAGE: ROBBIE EARLE — ONE OF THE ENGLISH CONTINGENT WHO HAVE BROUGHT A LEVEL OF PROFESSIONALISM TO JAMAICAN FOOTBALL.

OPPOSITE PAGE: JAMAICA'S ENGLISH-BORN MIDFIELDER IS THEIR BEST-KNOWN PLAYER BUT HAS YET TO GUARANTEE HIMSELF A REGULAR FIRST-TEAM PLACE.

England
GASCOIGNE

'Gazza' was given his chance in the England team shortly before the 1990 World Cup. Since the previous year, the English media had been unanimous in demanding that Bobby Robson pick the precocious teenager, and when the England coach finally relented, the youngster took his chance to become one of the stars of Italia 90.

He has been the focus of media attention in his own country ever since and his tempestuous life-style has been carefully monitored. On the field, his career has been one of inconsistent form spattered with injuries. Lazio still saw fit to pay £5.5m for a player who had put himself out of action for a year with a hopeless tackle in the FA Cup Final, but then had to sell him on at a £1.5m loss. Since moving to Scotland however, the attention has not been so fierce and Gascoigne has found the time to marry a little more professional nous with his unique talent. His skill on the ball is second to none and whenever he beats an opponent with a drag-back, a flick or a casual nutmeg, he makes it look easy. But sometimes his tricks don't come off and he loses the ball. Given that he likes to play a lot of his game in his own half, this aspect of England's game could prove their Achilles Heel in a style of football that is much more reliant on keeping possession than has ever been seen before from a British team in the World Cup.

But Gazza is now one of the old heads in the squad and he is beginning to show a maturity that reflects that. Having failed to qualify for USA 94, he is far and away the most experienced player England have got at this level and the rest of the team will now be looking to their most famous star for direction as well as for inspiration. That he can turn a game in one moment of brilliance has never been in doubt. Whether he can accept the responsibilities of leadership at the highest level has yet to be seen.

FULL NAME:
Paul Gascoigne

BORN:
27.5.67

BIRTHPLACE:
Gateshead

HEIGHT:
1.79m/5ft 10in

WEIGHT:
79kg/12st 6lbs

CLUBS:
Newcastle United, Tottenham Hotspur, Lazio, Glasgow Rangers

DEBUT:
1990

❝ Daft as a brush. ❞
— *former England coach Bobby Robson*

DID YOU KNOW?
Gazza is the only survivor of the 1990 team that went out to Germany in the semi-finals.

THIS PAGE: PAUL GASCOIGNE — ENGLAND'S MAVERICK TALENT IS NOW THEIR MOST EXPERIENCED WORLD CUP PLAYER.

OPPOSITE PAGE: THE MOLDOVAN DEFENDERS SEEM TO BE GOING THE WRONG WAY AS GAZZA DOES HIS SHUFFLE AND ENGLAND WIN 4-0 ON SEPTEMBER 10TH, 1997.

Romania
HAGI

FULL NAME:
Gheorghe Hagi

BORN:
5.2.65

BIRTHPLACE:
Sacele

HEIGHT:
1.74m/5ft 1in

WEIGHT:
70kg/11st

CLUBS:
Constanta, Sportul Studentsec, Steaua Bucharest, Real Madrid, Brescia, Barcelona, Galatasaray

DEBUT:
1986

'The Maradona of the Carpathians' is an enigmatic figure. Having lifted his side to the top of their qualifying group for Italia 90, he was touted as the best player in the world, a man whose left foot was just as sweet as that of the Argentine legend Diego Maradona. The Romanians believed Hagi would be their key to success. The rest of the world waited with bated breath.

In the event, Hagi's contribution to that World Cup was minimal. He looked an average player in an average team. Although the Romanians scraped through to the second phase of the competition, they were largely unimpressive for a side thought to be in with the chance of winning the trophy. Hagi, their captain and star player, the kind of footballer who is expected to be able to win World Cups virtually single-handedly if necessary, missed their only victory in the finals. Far from repeating the heroics Maradona had performed four years previously, Hagi had nothing to show for his pre-tournament billing. It was little surprise when the Romanians were dumped out of the tournament on penalties by Eire in the second phase.

USA 94 was a different matter. Romania had finished on top of their qualifying group again and, this time, their captain inspired his team to first place in their finals group before masterminding the 3–2 defeat of Argentina in the second phase. Although teammate Ilie Dumitrescu got the plaudits that day, scoring twice and setting up the third, it was Hagi's influence in midfield that gelled the team and gave them the confidence for victory. He could have taken his team at least as far as the semi-finals had they not gone in a second successive penalty shoot-out, this time to Sweden.

The Romanians again qualified with ease for France 98, winning all their group games except the final 1–1 draw with Eire in which Hagi scored the opening goal. With their star player back on form again in Turkey, another World Cup on European soil could be enough for the Romanians to go all the way this time.

66 **He's got a great left foot. He could open a can of beans with that foot.** 99
— *former England goalkeeper Ray Clemence*

DID YOU KNOW?
Hagi is only the second Romanian player ever to win 100 caps.

THIS PAGE: GHEORGE HAGI — THE ROMANIANS WILL NEED THEIR CAPTAIN TO IMPROVE UPON HIS PREVIOUS WORLD CUP FORM IF THEY ARE TO LIVE UP TO EXPECTATIONS.

OPPOSITE PAGE: HAGI AT USA 94. COMMUNISM MEANT THAT *SATURDAY NIGHT FEVER* WASN'T SEEN IN ROMANIA FOR 15 YEARS AFTER ITS RELEASE.

Germany
HASSLER

A veteran of the 1990 World Cup who is still performing as consistently as ever at both club and international level. He looks slightly out of place in a team full of big men, but his lack of height is a great asset to the Germans. It gives him great pace over a couple of metres and that means he can squeeze into holes in the defence that his teammates can't get into. As a result, and for the benefit of his teammates, he is always scuttling around in the middle of the action, looking for an opening or closing down an opponent.

Hassler is one of the most mobile players on the German team. His role is to create havoc in midfield, whether his team are in possession or not. He is a tenacious tackler and has the energy when he wins the ball to pass it and move into a position where he can get it back. This means he makes a lot of dummy runs, taking markers with him, and giving other players the chance to penetrate the defence. But he is much more than a midfield terrier. His first touch rarely lets him down and he is a dangerous dead-ball merchant. The goal he scored against Bulgaria in 1996 from a free-kick on the edge of the area was typical of the precision with which he can pick out a ball-sized area of the goal that isn't properly guarded.

He also has the uncanny knack of scoring at the right time. Playing for his club in the 1996/97 UEFA Cup, Hassler scored two goals just before half-time to inspire his team to an early victory in the competition. He recently claimed two great goals in a qualifier against Armenia and while he continues to be such a threat in front of goal, it is unlikely that he will not be selected to play in his third World Cup.

FULL NAME:
Thomas Hassler

BORN:
30.5.66

BIRTHPLACE:
Berlin

HEIGHT:
1.66m/5ft 5in

WEIGHT:
67kg/10st 8lbs

CLUBS:
Köln, Karlsruhe

DEBUT:
1988

INTERNATIONAL HONOURS:
World Cup winner 1990, European Championships winner 1996

" A midfield magician. "
— *Agence France Presse*

DID YOU KNOW?
Hassler played the last time Germany lost, 1–0, in a friendly against France on January 6th, 1996.

THIS PAGE: THOMAS HASSLER — CREATIVE FORCE IN A TEAM THAT ALWAYS COMES GOOD FOR THE BIG OCCASION.

OPPOSITE PAGE: THE CATALYST IN THE GERMAN MIDFIELD PUTS HIS FOOT ON THE BALL AGAINST ALBANIA IN QUALIFYING.

FULL NAME:
Paul Emerson Carlyle Ince

BORN:
21.10.67

BIRTHPLACE:
Ilford

HEIGHT:
1.82m/6ft

WEIGHT:
73kg/11st 7lbs

CLUBS:
West Ham, Manchester United,
Inter Milan, Liverpool

DEBUT:
1993

The London East-End boy known as 'the Guv'nor' and the first black man to captain England grew up with his great aunt in Dagenham, after his father left home when he was two and his mother later emigrated to Germany. The battling defensive midfielder was first spotted playing football by West Ham coach John Lyall when he was 12 and signed for the Hammers as a YTS trainee at 14. Throughout his apprenticeship, he was made to work hard on improving his stamina and a bigger, stronger Paul Ince was then offered professional terms in July 1985.

Four years later he moved to Manchester United and fans of the East London club still haven't forgiven him for putting on Manchester's red shirt for a photo-shoot while he was still officially a West Ham player. He played over 200 times for the Red Devils and his performances earned him a call-up to the England squad. Inter Milan then paid £8m for him in 1995, but this was where it started to go wrong and a brilliant young career threatened to go into free-fall. He started picking up disciplinary cards at Inter and moved one reporter to suggest sarcastically that he be charged for a ticket to the San Siro, so little did he think of the Englishman's contribution to the team effort. He also lost his England place under Terry Venables at this time, after dropping out of the Umbro Cup squad.

Typically, he fought back at his critics with some improved performances in the New Year to gain the respect of the fans and the press, and after spending one more season in Italy, he returned to his homeland in 1997 to join Liverpool. At Anfield, he was immediately appointed captain and wasted no time in making himself indispensable to the team.

He is in the same position at international level and captained the team that drew in Rome to qualify for France. He is the perfect foil for Paul Gascoigne (see page 127) and his ability in front of goal is improving all the time.

> 66 **When a year goes by and you don't even get called into an England squad, you do begin to worry.** 99
> *— Paul Ince*

DID YOU KNOW?
Ince's first goal at the San Siro stadium was a spectacular overhead kick as Inter thrashed Padova 8–2.

THIS PAGE: PAUL INCE — SEEN HERE AGAINST ITALY IN ROME WEARING THE TRADITIONAL HEAD DRESS OF AN ENGLAND CAPTAIN.

OPPOSITE PAGE: HAS IMPROVED GREATLY AS AN ALL-ROUND PLAYER AFTER HIS EXPERIENCE IN SERIE A.

Stepping into Robert Prosinecki's (see page 154) boots at Red Star Belgrade when Prosinecki was going through a period of such awe-inspiring form was never going to be easy. But it eventually proved the making of Vladimir Jugovic in 1991. After a season playing alongside the golden boy of Croatian football in that prodigiously gifted side, Jugovic got his chance to shine when Spanish giants Real Madrid snapped up Prosinecki. In his first campaign as the club's first-choice midfield general, Jugovic guided Red Star to an unprecedented Championship and European Cup double, before joining the exodus of the nation's finest talent to Italy and Spain after the outbreak of civil war.

Since then, during silverware-laden spells with Sampdoria and Juventus, Jugovic has become recognized as one of the world's finest team players. He is always industrious, happy to adapt his style to play in a variety of positions, and is a reliable distributor of the ball. He can also pack a wicked shot. This summer he will finally be permitted to play on the stage his rich talents deserve.

The double Serie A title winner's move to Lazio from the famous Juve last year shocked the Italian football fraternity, with Juve coach Marcello Lippi admitting: 'I did try to stop Vladimir leaving, but to no avail. For me, Jugovic is an important player, a capable and competitive professional who has a lot to offer.'

That much was evident in Yugoslavia's World Cup qualifying campaign, when tireless running and aggressive ball-winning from their most gifted playmaker ground out several important victories. Goals in the 8–1 demolition of the Faeroe Islands, and also in the 5–0 drubbing meted out to Malta, highlighted his instinct to push forward whenever the occasion allows. Still only 28, he is blessed with a level of international experience that is rare among his compatriots. The reassembling of so many players from his Red Star days for France 98 gives Jugovic the opportunity to show exactly what European club and international football lost when Yugoslavia fell into civil war.

FULL NAME:
Vladimir Jugovic

BORN:
30.8.69

BIRTHPLACE:
Trstenik, Serbia

HEIGHT:
1.79m/5ft 10in

WEIGHT:
75kg/11st 11lbs

CLUBS:
Red Star Belgrade, Sampdoria, Juventus, Lazio

DEBUT:
1991

66 **Those who have gone abroad have benefited from competing in Europe's top leagues.** 99
— *Vladimir Jugovic*

DID YOU KNOW?
When Jugovic transferred to Sampdoria in June 1992, the Italian FA due to United Nations sanctions on Yugoslavia, froze his transfer fee.

THIS PAGE: VLADIMIR JUGOVIC — THAT HE SUCCESSFULLY REPLACED PROSINECKI AT RED STAR IS TESTAMENT TO THIS MAN'S ABILITY.

OPPOSITE PAGE: THE COMPLETE MIDFIELDER — HARD-RUNNING IN DEFENCE, INSPIRATIONAL IN ATTACK.

FULL NAME:
Osvaldo Giraldo Junior

BORN:
22.2.73

BIRTHPLACE:
Sao Paolo

HEIGHT:
1.68m/5ft 6in

WEIGHT:
60kg/9st 6lbs

CLUBS:
Ituano, São Paolo, Middlesbrough, Atletico Madrid

DEBUT:
1993

> 66 **He wants to be the best player in the world.** 99
> — *former coach Bryan Robson*

DID YOU KNOW?
Middlesbrough have the first option to buy Juninho back when he leaves Atletico Madrid.

THIS PAGE: JUNINHO — PICTURED HERE DURING HIS TIME ON TEESSIDE.

OPPOSITE PAGE: HIS MOVE TO ATLETICO REJUVENATED HIS INTERNATIONAL PROSPECTS.

Bryan Robson, the former England captain and coach of newly-promoted Middlesbrough in the English Premiership, spent the entire summer of 1995 tracking down Juninho. The Brazilian had won the World Club Championship with São Paolo in 1994 and was the current Brazilian Player of the Year when Robson surprised the football world by finally persuading him to join the Boro in October.

Middlesbrough paid São Paolo £4.75m for the services of their biggest new star, but within ten minutes of his league debut against Leeds United, it was obvious that the English club had got a bargain. Juninho picked the ball up on the halfway line, cut inside the Leeds defence from the left, and delivered a defence-splitting pass for Norwegian international Jan Age Fjortoft to score the first goal. It was the kind of trick the Brazilian would reproduce on many occasions, delivering the final pass for a teammate, or adding the variation of sprinting forward himself to receive a return pass. He is very pacy and tough on the ball, and a master of the quick one-two.

He was so effective in his midfield role for Middlesbrough that shortly before he left England for Spain, football statisticians at Opta Index calculated that Juninho was the Premiership's most effective player. He was certainly Middlesbrough's best player in his time there, despite a team that included Fabrizio Ravanelli (see page 66) and two of Juninho's compatriots in Emerson and the 1994 World Cup winner Branco. Typically, Juninho dedicated the award made to him by the statisticians to his club's fans, 'who are the best in the world'.

Juninho won a lot of friends in his time in England, through his football and through his courtesy and geniality off the pitch, before his transfer to Spanish League and Cup double-winners Atletico Madrid. When the Boro were relegated, Juninho was honest enough to admit that he would have to be moving on for the sake of his career. And sure enough, after his move to Madrid, it wasn't long before he found himself being recalled to the Brazilian squad by Coach Mario Zagallo.

Norway
LEONARDSEN

An attacking midfielder with considerable flair, Leonardsen wasted no time in making a name for himself in the English Premiership, where he is now widely considered to be one of the most effective players in the league. He is deceptively strong, his passing is reliably accurate and his consistent goalscoring record from midfield is testament to a hard shot that is all too often on target. His willingness to attack defenders and get forward also makes him one of the most immediately noticeable players in the Norwegian team.

Leonardsen had begun his career at lowly Clausengen, but nine goals in 64 appearances for Molde made him worthy of a £100,000 price tag when he transferred to Rosenborg. A further 20 goals in 63 games there caused that evaluation to multiply six fold by the time Wimbledon moved in for their player. Rosenborg were happy and so were Wimbledon. Leonardsen comfortably made the step up to the English Premiership. During a brief loan period he scored in a 4–3 victory over Aston Villa and was immediately signed to the London club. He subsequently became their Player of the Year in his first season there and scored a total of 13 goals for Wimbledon. The fee paid for this scintillating midfielder had again proved a bargain and the London club made a killing when they sold him on to Liverpool for £3.5m.

But while it took astute Wimbledon manager Joe Kinnear to introduce this prodigious talent to the English game, Leonardsen was far from an unknown in his native Norway. He was a member of the 1989 Youth World Cup squad and has since played for the national team at every level, making his full international debut at the age of just 19. Meanwhile, at club level, he won three successive Norwegian Championships with Rosenborg in 1992, 1993 and 1994. With teammate Erik Mykland (see page 146), Oeyvind Leonardsen is another example of the way the Norwegians have transformed in recent years from a dour long-ball outfit into a team that can keep the ball on the grass and still compete with the world's best.

FULL NAME:
Oeyvind Leonardsen

BORN:
17.8.70

BIRTHPLACE:
Kristiansund

HEIGHT:
1.76m/5ft 9in

WEIGHT:
71kg/11st 2lbs

CLUBS:
Clausengen, Molde, Rosenborg, Wimbledon, Liverpool

DEBUT:
1989

> 66 **He's one of the best players I ever signed.** 99
> — *Wimbledon manager*
> *Joe Kinnear*

DID YOU KNOW?
His goal against Switzerland in qualifying was the one that put Norway top of their group, where they stayed for the rest of the campaign.

THIS PAGE: OEYVIND LEONARDSEN — PERHAPS THE MOST TALENTED BALL PLAYER IN NORWAY'S NEW-LOOK TEAM.

OPPOSITE PAGE: LEONARDSEN BATTLES WITH CURRENT CLUB COLLEAGUE PHIL BABB AS NORWAY PLAY EIRE.

Bulgaria
LETCHKOV

FULL NAME:
Yordan Letchkov

BORN:
9.7.67

BIRTHPLACE:
Sliven

HEIGHT:
1.78m/5ft 10in

WEIGHT:
73kg/11st 7lbs

CLUBS:
Sliven, CSKA Sofia, Hamburg,
Marseilles, Besiktas

DEBUT:
1989

Thanks to their marauding midfielder's unstoppable run to hit the dynamite header that knocked out the Germans at USA 94, Bulgaria came within one game of the World Cup Final. That goal is now remembered as one of the greatest of the tournament. Not just for its importance, but for the move that preceded it. It was the culmination of some great teamwork against one of the tournament's favourites. It also capped the Bulgarians' midfield general's massive contribution to his country's first serious World Cup challenge. His was the fulcrum of the team and a lot of their better passing moves went through him.

The industrious midfielder whose balding pate scored that headed goal is still at the heart of Bulgaria's ambition to go one game further this time around. A commanding figure who directs the team from the centre-circle, Letchkov has been a regular in the national side for the best part of a decade now. He is a very industrious player who is always looking to get involved. He is still playing his club football at the very highest level, the European Champions League, and he doesn't look like tiring yet.

Letchkov began his career at his local club Sliven in 1985, but a move to high profile CSKA in the nation's capital launched a career that took this vital and energetic player to two of the biggest clubs in Germany and France before his move to Turkey's Besiktas club at the end of last summer. The Turkish League runners-up needed to strengthen their squad for their European Champions League assault and also wanted to take advantage of their Football Federation's decision to permit four foreign nationals in its League teams, instead of the limit of three they had previously insisted on. Letchkov said he thought he could be 'very useful' to Besiktas when the club signed him on a two-year contract. He has kept his word. With Letchkov, the Turks have held their own in Europe, while Bulgaria have disposed of the highly ranked Russians in qualifying with rather more ease than the Italians could manage.

> 66 **The fact that Besiktas will be competing in the Champions League was instrumental in my decision to play here.** 99
> — *Yordan Letchkov*

DID YOU KNOW?
Letchkov scored two goals at USA 94.

THIS PAGE: YORDAN LETCHKOV — THE BULGARIAN STAR OF USA 94 RETURNS TO THE FRAY.

OPPOSITE PAGE: HIS QUICK AND DECISIVE MIDFIELD PLAY KEEPS THE BALL MOVING FOR BULGARIA.

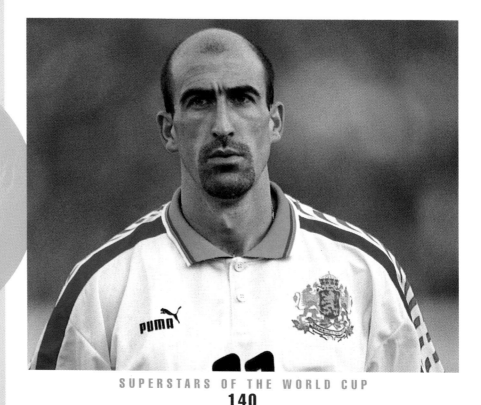

MIDFIELD
Scotland
MCALLISTER

FULL NAME:
Gary McAllister

BORN:
25.12.64

BIRTHPLACE:
Motherwell

HEIGHT:
1.86m/6ft 1in

WEIGHT:
78kg/12st 4lbs

CLUBS:
Motherwell, Leicester City,
Leeds United, Coventry City

DEBUT:
1990

66 **He's a great enthusiast. He'd approach a junior match with the same vigour he would an international.** 99
— *Motherwell coach Tommy McLean*

DID YOU KNOW?
McAllister is a great fan of England coach Glenn Hoddle and models his style on that of the former England international.

THIS PAGE: GARY MCALLISTER — MAY EVENTUALLY BE OUSTED BY DAVID HOPKIN IN THE SCOTLAND TEAM, BUT PERHAPS NOT JUST YET.

OPPOSITE PAGE: PLAYING THE CAPTAIN'S GAME IN THE VALUABLE DRAW IN VIENNA IN QUALIFYING, SEPTEMBER 31ST, 1996.

The experience of their captain and midfield playmaker is central to Scotland's hopes of getting past the first phase of a World Cup Finals for the first time in their history. He is an inspirational skipper whose international career is being extended thanks to his continuing form at club level.

Beginning his career in his home town, McAllister moved south to Leicester City for £100,000. He played over 200 games for the Midlands club, scoring 47 goals, before transferring to Leeds for £1m. In 231 games for Leeds, he netted a respectable 31 times. Now continuing his career in the English Premiership with struggling Coventry City, he is still one of the league's most consistent performers and regular goalscorers.

McAllister is a very precise striker of the ball who can place a 30-yard pass onto a teammate's foot with frightening regularity. These ball-playing skills are employed by coach Craig Brown in getting McAllister to take his team's penalties and many of their free-kicks.

Scotland fans will remember the penalty miss against England at Euro 96 that would have put the Scots back on level terms against their oldest rivals and kept them very much in the competition. In the event, that miss was followed by a swift counter-attack that culminated in an expertly taken goal by Paul Gascoigne (see page 127). That 2–0 defeat eventually saw the Scots out of the tournament, but they have kept faith in McAllister's ability and, even with John Collins (see page 112) in the side, he is still Scotland's best exponent in dead-ball situations.

After eight years at the centre of the Scottish midfield, there is speculation in Scotland that McAllister may soon lose his place to Leeds United's David Hopkin. The two are fairly similar in style, and if Scotland stick to a three-man midfield with Paul Lambert and John Collins , many believe that the captain's place in the starting line-up is under threat. But Hopkin, for all his talents, lacks the finesse of McAllister and the captain's skill and experience would be sorely missed. As the club form of this 33-year-old has yet to deteriorate, he is unlikely to be missing from Scotland's team in France.

South Africa
MOSHOEU

The man known as 'Shoes' for the masterful way he controls a football is a focal point of the South African team and one of the most technically gifted players in the world today. That he is still a relative unknown outside South Africa and Turkey is down to two reasons: he has never played for one of Europe's bigger clubs, and South Africa have only just re-entered the post-apartheid sports arena.

'Shoes' was rejected as a teenager by South Africa's biggest club, Kaizer Chiefs, and signed instead for his country's Second Division side, Blackpool. They promptly got promoted, and in their one season at the top level, a new star was born.

Promotion meant that he was in great demand but even after relegation he stayed at Blackpool to help them win promotion again. Kaizer Chiefs eventually signed him in 1993 but he played only 14 games for them before moving to Glenclerbirligi in Turkey. There he was sold to Kocaelispor for £800,000. This is a relatively small sum to pay for the frequent goals and the defence-splitting passes that make him a constant danger.

By the time South Africa were re-admitted to international football in 1992, he had broken his leg. This meant he didn't make his debut for the *Bafana Bafana* as the international team is known, until January 1993. He immediately made up for the delay with a goal in the friendly against Botswana. He has since followed that strike with several more and has become one of his team's greatest goalscoring threats, even though he usually operates from midfield. However, he can too often be ineffectual throughout an entire match, and the tight-marking that will be operating at France 98 will be the biggest test of his ability in his entire career to date.

FULL NAME:
John Lesiba Moshoeu

BORN:
18.12.65

BIRTHPLACE:
Diepkloof

HEIGHT:
1.77m/5ft 10in

WEIGHT:
68kg/10st 10lbs

CLUBS:
Diepkloof Blue Whales, Blackpool, Highlands Park, Kaizer Chiefs, Glenclerbirligi, Kocaelispor

DEBUT:
1993

INTERNATIONAL HONOURS:
African Nations Cup winner 1996

❝ Shoes is one of his team's greatest goalscoring threats even though he usually operates from midfield. ❞

DID YOU KNOW?
'Shoes' cost Kaizer Chiefs a club record £50,000 when he signed for them.

THIS PAGE: JOHN MOSHOEU — THE HERO OF THE TOWNSHIPS SEEN HERE REPRESENTING THE NEW SOUTH AFRICA AGAINST ENGLAND AT OLD TRAFFORD IN MAY 1997.

OPPOSITE PAGE: GREAT PLAYERS ALWAYS FIND THE TIME TO LOOK UP BEFORE PLAYING A PASS.

FULL NAME:
Erik Mykland

BORN:
21.7.71

BIRTHPLACE:
Kristiansund

HEIGHT:
1.72m/5ft 8in

WEIGHT:
63kg/9st 13lbs

CLUBS:
Bryne, Risor, Start Kristiansund,
Utrecht, FC Linz, Panathanaikos

DEBUT:
1990

The Norwegian side, for all their success and high FIFA ranking, are often criticized for playing an unattractive style of football that relies on an excessive number of long balls to tall, strong and aggressive front runners. This is still often true. They do play a more 'English' game than the English, but they have talented ball players now too. One of these is a mobile, creative midfielder who is the antithesis of that 'hoof it and hope' philosophy, Erik Mykland.

Mykland is a fantastic dribbler who is never scared to take defenders on and knows the exact moment to play perfectly weighted passes in behind the back line for his strikers to run onto. He is capable of buying a lot of time for his team whenever they are in possession by putting his foot on the ball in midfield and allowing his teammates to move into threatening positions. He is everywhere. A mark of his confidence, and a mark of his class, is that he is always looking for the ball.

Critics will say that Norway need more players like Mykland before they can challenge for the World Cup. They also point out that Norway's qualification group was probably the easiest in Europe, runners up Hungary were thrashed 7–1 at home by Yugoslavia in the first leg of their play-off, and Finland, Switzerland and Azerbaijan never threatened Mykland's team's position at the head of the group. But the Norwegians qualified unbeaten, demonstrating along the way that they could compete with the best by outpassing and outplaying a full-strength Brazilian team in a friendly in May of last year. Erik Mykland was the centrepiece of the team that day, as Norway ran out comfortable 4–2 victors. It was Mykland's unstoppable runs through the midfield that prompted his coach to say that the Brazilians were 'as organized as garbage' in the centre of the pitch. That wouldn't have been the case if Mykland hadn't torn them apart.

Norway have shown that they no longer have to depend on their strength and stamina to win football matches. The little man in the middle is the director of some of their better passing sequences.

> **"** Erik Mykland has technique and skill. He is one of the artists in the Norwegian team. **"**
> — *Nils Johan Samb, Norwegian coach after France 98*

DID YOU KNOW?
After Norway beat Brazil 4–2 in a friendly last summer, Romario asked for the name of this roving midfielder.

THIS PAGE: ERIK MYKLAND – THE NORWEGIAN PLAYMAKER IS STILL WEARING HIS USA 94 BEARD.

OPPOSITE PAGE: DEMONSTRATING THE BALANCE OF A WORLD-CLASS INTERNATIONAL

The man who scored against Turkey in his one appearance in Denmark's unsuccessful defence of the European Championship crown in 1996 is a highly versatile, all-round footballer who can be seen operating in and between both penalty areas. His presence in the Tottenham and Denmark midfields shores up the defensive side of their play as well as providing both teams with extra attacking options. He is a strong tackler who tracks back well to support his defence by picking up mobile midfielders, but he is also just as useful in attack. In possession, he is a stylish passer of the ball and also shows himself keen to get involved in attack by moving into spaces where he can receive the ball back again from his teammates. He rarely shies from an opportunity to get into goalscoring positions but whenever the attack breaks down, Neilsen is the first to regain his original place in midfield, where he harries and chases to prevent the opposition from mounting an effective attack.

Starting out by playing for his home town on the west coast of Denmark, he moved to the Bundesliga to play for Bayern Munich as a teenager but did not enjoy his time there, representing the Bavarian outfit in the first team on only one occasion. Returning to Denmark, he excelled in the midfield of the Brondby team that outplayed Liverpool in the 1995 UEFA Cup. Finally recognized in England, he was signed to Tottenham for £1m by new coach Gerry Francis, and has consistently looked one of the classiest new arrivals at the North London club.

Allan Neilsen has successfully made the step up to international football, demonstrating his importance to the team's efforts to qualify for France, not least in the pivotal role he assumed in the 4–0 destruction of Slovenia, when he scored twice and was outstanding throughout. He is now being widely touted in Denmark as the natural successor to the excellent Kim Vilfort at the heart of the national team's midfield. High praise indeed.

FULL NAME:
Allan Neilsen

BORN:
13.3.71

BIRTHPLACE:
Esbjerg

HEIGHT:
1.80m/5ft 11in

WEIGHT:
71kg/11st 2lbs

CLUBS:
Esbjerg, Bayern Munich, Odense,
FC Copenhagen, Brondby,
Tottenham

DEBUT:
1995

> 66 I'm pleased to be settled and I'm looking forward to playing. 99
> — Allan Neilsen on signing for Spurs

DID YOU KNOW?
Neilsen scored within a minute on his international debut after coming on as a substitute in the 2–0 Euro 96 qualifying win over Armenia.

THIS PAGE: ALAN NEILSEN — GREAT ALL-ROUND FOOTBALLER WHO PERSONIFIES DENMARK'S BLEND OF SKILL AND GRIT.

OPPOSITE PAGE: BRINGING THE BALL TO GROUND IN ATHENS LAST OCTOBER.

MIDFIELD
Nigeria
OKOCHA

The maverick of the Nigerian team is a very exciting attacking midfielder who likes to run at defenders with the ball. He is pacy and has the close control and dribbling abilities to get past the best markers in the world. He is a regular scorer for his club side and has also proved his goalscoring abilities by netting twice at the Olympics. Like many great individualistic ball players, however, he can be a little elaborate and his concentration on the ball sometimes diminishes his ability to see the easy pass to a teammate.

Okocha began his professional career in the university town of Enugu. After accepting a move to Germany to play in Neunkirchen, he moved on to Frankfurt in 1992. He has since joined his international teammate Okechukwu Uche (see page 224) at Fenerbahçe. This is the only Istanbul club based on the Asian side of the Bosphoros, the water separating European and Asian Istanbul. The club is fiercely Turkish and the pair have been encouraged to take Turkish citizenship and even to change their names. Okocha became Mohammed Yavuz Okacha, but is still known to fans around the world simply as Jay Jay.

In his first season in Turkey, he scored 16 goals to finish the season as the club's second top scorer behind striker Elvir Bolic. At the Olympics, he hit a cracking strike from the edge of the area for the opening goal in the 2–0 defeat of Mexico in the quarter-finals, having already scored against Japan earlier in the competition.

This is one player who has the potential to make quite a name for himself at France 98. In his red boots he is currently playing on the top of his form for his club and also has the experience of USA 94 behind him. If he is given space, that combination should put him in good stead for some confident performances in France. He is a critical figure for the Eagles, who will look to give him the ball and pray for a moment of magic from him to turn the game.

FULL NAME:
Augustine Azuka 'Jay Jay' Okocha

BORN:
14.08.73

BIRTHPLACE:
Ilorin, Kwara State

HEIGHT:
1.70m/5ft 7in

WEIGHT:
67kg/10st 8lbs

CLUBS:
Alyufsalam Rocks, Enugu Rangers, Borussia Neunkirchen, Eintracht Frankfurt, Fenerbahçe

INTERNATIONAL HONOURS:
African Nations Cup winner 1994

> 66 He has the wiles of Pelé and Maradona combined. 99
> — *eulogy in the Nigerian press*

DID YOU KNOW?
Okocha was threatened with legal action last summer after attacking two reporters who tried to photograph him with his girlfriend after a training session.

THIS PAGE: AUGUSTINE OKOCHA – 'JAY JAY' PREPARING TO START ANOTHER MATCH FOR HIS COUNTRY.

OPPOSITE PAGE: SHIELDING THE BALL FROM KENYA'S JOHN ODHIAMBO IN QUALIFYING.

Argentina
ORTEGA

Ever since *el burrito* (the little donkey) began to make his mark at River Plate, the Argentine press has been keen to liken him to Diego Maradona (see page 12). Ariel Ortega has undoubtedly been the most talented ball player in the Argentinian team since Maradona and his mazy dribbling has been the delight of their fans. But he has done what he can to dismiss any such comparisons, saying: 'Diego is unique', and that he doesn't expect there ever will be another player like him.

The comparison comes because Ortega began his international career as the linkman between midfield and attack, much the same position as Maradona used to play. But the man who now partners Romario (see page 68) at Valencia is more likely to be employed as an outright attacker up alongside Gabriel Batistuta (see page 22). Argentina rely on fast counter-attacking, and Ortega's love affair with the ball, while beautiful to watch, runs contrary to their strategy of quick one-touch play in the attacking half of the pitch. But as long as he is playing most of his football in the opposition's penalty area, the ability to hang onto the ball is always a boon.

Although he has yet to become a real hit in Spain, Ortega may still prove to be one of the greatest players of France 98. He certainly has the talent and is obviously a player who relishes the big occasion. His performance as Argentina defeated Chile 2–1 in Santiago to claim their place in France was quite brilliant. He dominated the game, setting up Gallardo for the first goal with a perfect cross from the right in the first half, and playing a crucial part in the build-up that led to the winning goal from Lopez.

His silky skills are the perfect counter-point to the brash and hard-hitting style of his fellow striker. It is just possible that, with the maverick Ortega weaving his magic in the danger area, the Argentinians may have found the necessary touch of genius to lift them above the competition, just as they had in Kempes (see page 10) in 1978 and in Maradona in 1986.

FULL NAME:
Ariel Arnaldo Ortega

BORN:
4.3.74

BIRTHPLACE:
Libertador General San Martín, Jujuy

HEIGHT:
1.82m/6ft

WEIGHT:
76kg/12st

CLUBS:
River Plate, Valencia

DEBUT:
1994

❝ Ariel Ortega, a wonder of magic and beauty in the Santiago night. ❞
— *Argentine press after qualification was assured in the Chilean capital*

DID YOU KNOW?
Ortega played for River Plate for five and a half years, scoring 32 goals before moving to Valencia in 1997.

THIS PAGE: ARNALDO ORTEGA — THE NEW MARADONA? COMPARISONS ARE UNFAIR, BUT HE IS A BIT GOOD.

OPPOSITE PAGE: CHALLENGING FOR THE BALL AGAINST PERU IN THE RIVER PLATE STADIUM IN QUALIFYING.

A member of the Yugoslavian national team at Italia 90, Robert Prosinecki is a dead-ball expert who can also score goals in open play with either foot. He is the charismatic figure at the centre of the Croatian midfield, and his mere presence can lift those playing around him. It was for these reasons that FC Croatia, the club formerly known as Dinamo Zagreb, were so keen to bring Prosinecki back home from Spain. They believed that with their inspirational midfielder back in the ranks, they would be able to attract other Croatian internationals back home and eventually recreate the national team at club level. The irony of this is that Dinamo Zagreb, under Coach Miroslav Blazevic, had rejected Prosinecki as a youngster, selling the player to Red Star Belgrade. Blazevic was later to come across his former club player in the international set-up after the coach took over the national side and Prosinecki had proved his worth to Red Star.

Prosinecki became a World U-18 Champion with Yugoslavia in 1987, along with compatriots Davor Suker (see page 85) and Zvonimir Boban (see page 109). But unlike his teammates, Prosinecki also won three Yugoslav championships and the European Cup with Red Star. But when he first went abroad, he started to become plagued by injuries and at first had quite a difficult period in Spain, finding himself on the treatment table for a lot of his time in the Spanish capital. At Euro 96, he again had to leave the field in the quarter-final encounter with Portugal after picking up an injury in the first half.

So, after spells at three Spanish League clubs, Prosinecki is back playing in the Croatian capital where he began his career. There is a certain patriotic fervour about the Croatian national team at the moment, and in the light of the nation's recent history, this highly talented side may just have the edge on many of their opponents this summer. Although no player in France will need to be encouraged to pick up his game for the World Cup.

FULL NAME:
Robert Prosinecki

BORN:
12.1.69

BIRTHPLACE:
Schwenningen, Germany

HEIGHT:
1.82m/6ft

WEIGHT:
76kg/12st

CLUBS:
Dinamo Zagreb (now FC Croatia), Red Star Belgrade, Real Madrid, Oviedo, Barcelona, Seville, FC Croatia

DEBUT:
1994

66 I have come home and I am pleased to be back. 99
— Robert Prosinecki

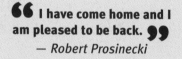

DID YOU KNOW?
The Yugoslavian Federation tried to block Prosinecki's transfer to Madrid as he was not yet 25 years old.

THIS PAGE: ROBERT PROSINECKI — HIS RETURN TO CROATIA IS A SYMBOL OF NATIONALISTIC PRIDE.

OPPOSITE PAGE: CROATIA'S PLAYMAKER HAS THE UNUSUAL DISTINCTION OF REPRESENTING TWO COUNTRIES AT WORLD CUP LEVEL — THE FORMER YUGOSLAVIA IN 1990, AND NOW CROATIA.

S pain's indomitable pillar of defence goes by a name that translates as 'iron', which is quite apt. He made his international debut as a 21-year-old and has since become part of the spine of the team. He has an extremely powerful shot that is often used to take free-kicks, where his 'hit-it-and-hope' tactics contrast well with the more cunning tricks of his teammates.

Coach Javier Clemente has said that he respects what he calls the 'English game' and that he tries to get his team to play that way. His first-choice stopper looks like the archetypal English defender. Strong in the air and hard on the ground, his presence in the opposition penalty area at corners and free-kicks is always a cause for concern. But despite assuming the role of 'big man at the back', Hierro Ruiz is blessed with unusual ball skills for a man of his size, and he began his career as a creative midfield player. He still comes forward whenever possible but is nowadays more likely to play at the back, especially for the national team, where his understanding with goalkeeper Zubizarreta (see page 255) is remarkable, given that they have never played together at club level.

The Andaluz is another player who has been given an extended high-salary contract at Real Madrid. He has now signed up until 2003, when he will be 35, and has made it clear that he is quite happy to spend the rest of his playing days with Real. His club coach Fabio Capello rates him as 'one of the best two or three players in Europe'. This is no idle bravado from a coach trying to build up his defender's reputation. Former Barcelona coach Bobby Robson also recognized Hierro as 'the best all-round defender in the League'. He is playing at the top of his career and could walk into any team playing at the finals. Like Zubizarreta, this will probably be his last World Cup and he will be keen to make it a memorable one.

FULL NAME:
Fernando Hierro Ruiz

BORN:
23.3.68

BIRTHPLACE:
Velez-Malaga

HEIGHT:
1.87m/6ft 2in

WEIGHT:
82kg/12st 13lbs

CLUBS:
Torre del Mar, Velez CF,
Atletico Malagueno, Valladolid,
Real Madrid

DEBUT:
1989

66 **I'm getting the attitude of an out-and-out defender.** 99
— *Fernando Hierro Ruiz*

DID YOU KNOW?
Coach Javier Clemente considers him the best player in the world.

THIS PAGE: FERNANDO HIERRO RUIZ — WITH HIS LEADERSHIP QUALITIES, THE SPANISH HOPE TO TAKE THE WORLD CUP BACK HOME OVER THE PYRENEES.

OPPOSITE PAGE: ANOTHER POWERFUL SURGE FROM THE BACK AGAINST THE FAEROE ISLANDS IN THE FINAL QUALIFIER.

The hub around which the Dutch attackers rotate is this Surinamese-born defensive midfielder who has been part of the set-up ever since making his international debut at the age of 18. While he was still a teenager, the Dutch League and Cup winner became the nation's great black hope, but leaving Holland so young looked like being the undoing of an extraordinarily promising career.

He is a very industrious midfielder whose sheer work-rate permits those around him to concentrate more on attack. His tireless contribution to the team-effort is integral to the Dutch system of closing people down as soon as they receive possession, and whenever he wins the ball, he shields it well and makes it very hard to get it back. This skill allows the Dutch to keep possession in crowded areas.

By the standards he had set himself at Ajax since making his first team debut at 16 and becoming a European Cup winner at 19, Seedorf didn't have a good first season abroad. That his loss of form in Italy had affected his confidence was obvious in a series of unconvincing performances for Holland at Euro 96 the following summer. His most noticeable contribution to the cause was to miss a penalty in the quarter-final shoot-out against France. With that unfortunate conclusion, one of the pre-tournament favourites went out of the competition.

At Real Madrid he has found his form and confidence again, and the £3.5m they paid for him is beginning to look like a bargain. He is being given a roving role there and is responsible for shoring up the centre-circle as well as for maintaining the goalscoring records of his teammates Raul Gonzalez Blanco (see page 26), Davor Suker (see page 85), and Mijatovic (see page 57). The more glamorous side of his job involves making surging runs into the area where his strength is enough to shake off the most aggressive markers. And if Holland are winning with seconds to go, expect to see Clarence Seedorf with the ball down by the corner flag, fiercely holding off two defenders and playing out time.

FULL NAME:	
Clarence Seedorf	
BORN:	
1.4.76	
BIRTHPLACE:	
Paramaribo, Surinam	
HEIGHT:	
1.76m/5ft 9in	
WEIGHT:	
76kg/12st	
CLUBS:	
AS '80, Real Almere, Ajax, Sampdoria, Real Madrid	
DEBUT:	
1994	

> **He must rank as one of the most effective midfielders in Europe.**
> — *Spanish international Rafael Alkorta*

DID YOU KNOW?
Seedorf threatened to quit the team when he was substituted after just 25 minutes of the Euro 96 encounter with Switzerland.

THIS PAGE: CLARENCE SEEDORF — A MAJOR PART OF HOLLAND'S QUALIFICATION FOR EURO 96 AND FRANCE 98.

OPPOSITE PAGE: AVOIDING THE ATTENTIONS OF FRANCE'S ZINEDINE ZIDANE.

Argentina
SIMEONE

FULL NAME:
Diego Pablo Simeone

BORN:
28.4.70

BIRTHPLACE:
Capital Federal

HEIGHT:
1.88m/6ft 2in

WEIGHT:
82kg/12st 13lbs

CLUBS:
Velez Sarsfield, Pisa, Sevilla,
Atletico Madrid, Inter Milan

DEBUT:
1990

INTERNATIONAL HONOURS:
Copa America winner 1991

❝ I am not a violent player. ❞
— *Diego Simeone*

DID YOU KNOW?
Hooligans surrounded Diego
Simeone, and stole his boots from
his bag as he came out of a press
conference in Buenos Aires
in the summer of 1997.

THIS PAGE: DIEGO SIMEONE — ARGENTINA'S
GREAT DEFENSIVE PLAYER CELEBRATES
A RARE GOAL.

OPPOSITE PAGE: ARGENTINA'S HARD MAN
COME FORWARD WITH THE BALL.

Argentina's regimented style of football demands under Daniel Passarella that its players act as cogs in a wheel. Each performs a specific function and rarely, with the exception of Daniel Ortega (see page 153), will you see moments of isolated brilliance from any of their players. Hard-hitting midfielder Diego Simeone is very much a player who serves the structure of the unit. Rarely flamboyant, his contribution to the team effort is not immediately noticeable, but recent history has shown that when he isn't suspended, he is an automatic choice on the right side of Argentina's midfield. He understands the Argentinian game well, receiving the ball from defence and moving it along quickly with the minimum of fuss.

One of Argentina's USA 94 veterans, Diego Simeone made his Velez Sarsfield debut at the age of 17 and immediately became a regular in the side. He served a three-year apprenticeship there, before moving to Europe. Since that time, this reliable team player has gained a lot of invaluable experience in both Italy and Spain, as well as in the World Cup finals of 1994. He spent two seasons at both Pisa and Seville before the 1994 World Cup, moving up to the Spanish capital immediately afterwards, where he played for a three further seasons before signing for Inter Milan last summer.

Simeone is more likely to make a name for himself on the disciplinary charts than on the goalscoring charts in France. He is not a player you can expect to see making bold runs in behind the defence. Nor will he excite the fans by taking defenders on with the ball. This no-nonsense hardman plays the percentages. If a short pass will do the job, that's what he'll give. He likes to play rather more of a static role than that of a flying winger. He holds his position and knocks quick balls to teammates' feet. It's an unglamorous job, but it makes this highly experienced midfielder one of the most quietly effective players on the team, and a crucial part of coach Daniel Passarella's set-up.

Colombia
VALDERRAMA

The mad-haired maestro in the middle of Colombia's midfield, like most of the old guard, missed last summer's Copa America, but it was significant that his team played the entire tournament without using his number ten shirt. Their captain was probably getting bored of the Copa America anyway. He had played in each of the five tournaments between 1987 and 1997, earning praise for his contribution in each one. He also played in both the 1990 and 1994 World Cups, scoring the second goal in Colombia's 2–0 win over the United Arab Emirates at Italia 90. And although he is now nearly 37, Valderrama looks far from the end of his usefulness at international level. This will almost certainly be his last World Cup, but he will be much more than an experienced squad player in France.

Three days before his 36th birthday, he orchestrated Tampa Bay's 4–0 defeat of New England Revolution in the MLS, providing the final assist for each of the four goals. Some might think this sounds like the feat of a good player seeing out the remainder of his career in a lucrative but mediocre league. But *el pibe* (the boy) had collected his 100th cap in a friendly against the Jamaican national team in Kingston less than a month before that MLS match, and a week after his birthday, he captained the Colombians to World Cup qualification with a 1–0 win over neighbours Venezuela in Barranquilla.

It doesn't matter that Valderrama will be one of the oldest players competing in France. His game has never been about work-rate and stamina. His talent is that he can keep the ball. Despite the attentions of the world's best defenders, it is usually the man in the yellow shirt with the shock of orange hair who comes out of the midfield melée with the ball at his feet. He is not a prolific goalscorer, but his passing is invariably superb and the wealth of experience he has to share with his colleagues will be invaluable to the Colombians as they try to improve upon their showing at USA 94.

FULL NAME:
Carlos Alberto Valderrama Palacio

BORN:
2.9.61

BIRTHPLACE:
Santa Marta

HEIGHT:
1.78m/5ft 10in

WEIGHT:
73kg/11st 7lbs

CLUBS:
Atletico Junior, Tampa Bay Mutiny

DEBUT:
1985

> 66 Before I played against him, I thought he was a bit lazy, a luxury player, but you try getting the ball off him. It took three of us at one point. 99
> — *England defender Graeme Le Saux*

DID YOU KNOW?
Valderrama has been voted South American Player of the Year three times.

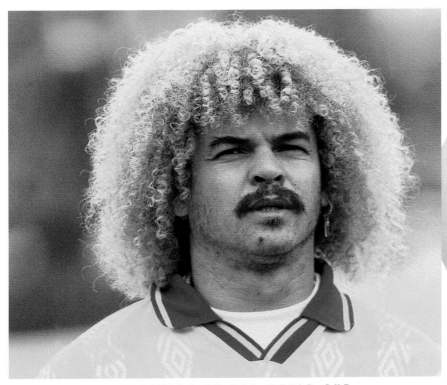

THIS PAGE: VALDERRAMA – 36 YEARS OLD AND STILL GOING STRONG.

OPPOSITE PAGE: THE ELDER STATESMAN OF COLOMBIAN FOOTBALL IS STILL THE PIVOT OF THE TEAM.

Austria
VASTIC

FULL NAME:
Ivica Vastic

BORN:
20.9.69

BIRTHPLACE:
Split

HEIGHT:
1.79m/5ft 10in

WEIGHT:
78kg/12st 4lbs

CLUBS:
NK Split, Vienna,
St Polten, Admiral Wacker,
MSV Duisburg, Sturm Graz

DEBUT:
1996

66 **Everybody's
really nice here.** 99
— *Ivica Vastic back at the Austrian
camp in qualifying*

DID YOU KNOW?
Vastic's father played up front for
Sarajevo, Hajduk Split and Varazdin
in the 1960s.

THIS PAGE: IVICA VASTIC — A RELATIVE
UNKNOWN OUTSIDE AUSTRIA, SO FAR.

OPPOSITE PAGE: EQUALLY AS EFFECTIVE AS
A GOAL PROVIDER AND AS A GOALSCORER,
VASTIC COULD WELL BE ONE OF THE HEROES
OF FRANCE 98.

The Austrians have been waiting for a player like the Croatian-born Ivica Vastic to come along for quite some time. For years they had been unable to find an able foil for their leading marksman Toni Polster (see page 65), but now the blossoming understanding between Vastic and Polster is one of the more awesome aspects of this new Austrian team. The Sturm Graz playmaker-cum-striker's link-up play with the Cologne veteran was at the heart of many of Austria's most impressive displays during the qualifiers. This skilful front-runner with dazzling close control can sit in behind the Polster and play enticing balls through to the goalscorer all day long. Although Vastic himself hit the net just once in qualifying, in the 2–0 home win over Estonia, his overall contribution to the cause earned justifiable praise and a regular place in the first team.

Born in Croatia, Vastic would probably have played for his native country at Euro 96, but having taken out Austrian citizenship in December 1995, he decided to throw his lot in with his adopted country. As he happened to be the Austrian Bundesliga's leading marksman at the time, national coach Herbert Prohaska had no hesitation in throwing Vastic straight into the fray. The new frontman made the impressive debut everybody expected in a 1–0 friendly victory over Switzerland in March 1996.

Now established in Austria's starting line-up, and buoyed by a second successive cup winners' medal for his club last season, Vastic has continued his prolific form through 1997/98. At the halfway stage of the season, his goal making and scoring talents had helped open a nine-point gap between his club and their nearest Austrian Bundesliga challengers, Grazer AK. It also gave them a whopping 12-point lead over third-placed Austria Vienna. Should this bright footballer's form continue, it's likely that Vastic will arrive in France having inspired his club to their first-ever Austrian Bundesliga title in 89 years. Can he do the same for his country? Well, the Austrians have as good a chance as they've had for a long time, so only the games will tell.

MIDFIELD
France
ZIDANE

FULL NAME:
Zinedine Zidane

BORN:
23.6.72

BIRTHPLACE:
Marseille

HEIGHT:
1.85m/6ft 8in

WEIGHT:
80kg/12st 7lbs

CLUBS:
Cannes, Bordeaux, Juventus

DEBUT:
1994

❝ I must dribble as little as possible; one, two, three touches. No more. ❞
— *Zidane*

DID YOU KNOW?
Zidane nearly turned down Juve, as the 'thought of playing in Italy was scary'.

THIS PAGE: ZINEDINE ZIDANE — ALL-ROUND ABILITY AND COMMITMENT HAVE MADE HIM A REGULAR STARTER IN THE HOST TEAM.

OPPOSITE PAGE: BREAKING FORWARD WITH THE BALL AGAINST BRAZIL IN LE TOURNOI.

Zidane is a tall, strong, skilful and extremely inventive player who likes to get forward regularly to score his fair share of goals from midfield. He made his international debut after France had failed to qualify for USA 94 when he came on for the injured Youri Djorkaeff to score the two goals that earned his team a draw. He modestly says that he only played because Djorkaeff was injured, but it has come as no surprise to see that he has become an integral part of the French national team ever since.

The man who learned his incredible dribbling skills in the streets of Marseilles has now become an idol in France, where he is often compared to the great Michel Platini (see page 94). He is also popular in Italy, having created two goals and scored a superb individual effort against Ajax to take Juve to the 1997 UEFA Cup Final in a 4–1 victory which prompted Ajax coach Louis van Gaal to say: 'Zidane was a different class, even in such a remarkable team as this Juventus.'

Zidane also helped Juve win the World Club Cup that year by flicking a corner on for man-of-the-match Alessandro Del Piero to score the winner. Add the European Super Cup and Italian League to his expanding list of honours and you begin to realize that any player who can shine in such a great club side as Juve must be special indeed.

He says he prefers to play alongside the midfielder of Armenian stock he replaced on the night of his debut, though it remains to be seen whether the latter will start from a squad that contains Christophe Dugarry (see page 34) and Florian Maurice (see page 53). But one thing is sure, 'Zizou', if fit, will play. Although he was very quiet in Euro 96 when coach Aime Jacquet was heavily criticized for not including Eric Cantona and David Ginola in the squad, the decision to stand by the player Jacquet considered to have been instrumental in getting the team to England in the first place has since been vindicated.

Zidane's record shows that he can turn a game on his own and, along with club teammate Didier Deschamps (see page 120), he will hope to celebrate his 26th birthday by being the inspiration behind what promises to be the most awesome midfield competing this summer.

NAME:
Bobby Moore

COUNTRY:
England

WORLD CUPS:
1966, 1970

England's World Cup winning captain's cool temperament and impeccable timing in the tackle were inspirational in a decade notorious for on-field violence.

NAME:
Daniel Passarella

COUNTRY:
Argentina

WORLD CUPS:
1978, 1982

A great marshall and an uncompromising central defender who captained his country to victory in 1978 before going on to manage them.

NAME:
Rune Bratseth

COUNTRY:
Norway

WORLD CUPS:
1994

An extremely fast and tight central defender who led Norway to their first ever finals at USA 94.

NAME:
Franceschino Baresi

COUNTRY:
Italy

WORLD CUPS:
1986, 1990, 1994

After Franco tried to retire in 1992, Italy's drop in form persuaded this visionary organizer to return for USA 94. Hard and often fair.

NAME:
Paul McGrath

COUNTRY:
Eire

WORLD CUPS:
1990, 1994

An extremely talented all-rounder who was the rock upon which Jack Charlton's Irish team was built.

TACTICAL INNOVATIONS

LE VERROU (SWISS BOLT)

1-3-3-3

In the 1950s, Swiss coach Karl Rappan started the fashion of dropping a fourth defender in to 'sweep' behind the centre-back whenever they lost the ball. His team closed down the opposition by outnumbering them in all areas before breaking quickly. 'Le verrou' required great fitness, but it worked.

THE GREATEST

NAME:
Franz Beckenbauer

COUNTRY:
West Germany

BORN:
11.9. 45

BIRTHPLACE:
Munich

WORLD CUPS:
1966, 1970, 1974

CAPS:
103 (13 goals)

MOMENT OF GLORY

When West Germany became champions for the second time in 1990, Beckenbauer became the first man to win the World Cup both as player and as coach. 'The Kaiser' first appeared as a right-half at England 66, scoring four goals on the way to the final, where he marked Bobby Charlton. He returned to torment the English in Mexico 70, scoring the first in his side's remarkable comeback from 2–0 down to win their quarter-final match.

He is best remembered for the sweeper role he played at the 1974 finals. His ability to initiate attacks from deep was at the centrepiece of the side that met the Dutch in one of the most exhilarating World Cup finals ever played. By Argentina 78, Beckenbauer had retired from international football and was playing for New York Cosmos in the fledgling US league but he returned as national coach in 1986, despite the fact that he had never been on any of the German Federation's supposedly obligatory management courses. In Mexico and in Italy, he took West Germany to the final, managing as he had always played: concentrating on defence but ever poised to switch to attack at the right moment.

Strengthening the centre of defence by dropping an early version of the sweeper back to cover deep

FULL NAME:
Tony Adams

BORN:
10.10.66

BIRTHPLACE:
Romford

HEIGHT:
1.86m/6ft 1in

WEIGHT:
77kg/12st 2lbs

CLUBS:
Arsenal

DEBUT:
1987

When the England and Arsenal stalwart first came to prominence at the age of 20, he was considered to be the greatest prospect England had at the time and many considered him to have the potential to become their best ever defender. However, with the exception of the current claimant to that title, Bobby Moore (see page 168), English central defenders have always had the reputation for being strong in the air and in the tackle but embarrassingly inferior on the ball. Allow the world's best attackers to run at them with the ball and they would be left standing, bewildered by the sheer pace and skill of their opponents. And if they ever did get close enough to win a tackle, their only tactic would be to punt a long, hopeful ball up the wing where a full-back would invariably collect it to start another siege on the England goal.

For a long time, Tony Adams seemed to fit this stereotypical description perfectly. Always good in the air and a well-used tool at set-pieces, a string of unconvincing performances earned him the nickname of 'donkey' earlier in his career. He was never as bad as he was made out to be, but he is certainly better now than he ever was. Whether the arrival at Highbury of players like Dennis Bergkamp (see page 25) has taught him a thing or two about kicking a football is open to speculation. Whether his public announcement of his alcoholism and his subsequent private battle to fight it has anything to do with his recent improvement is also unsure, but his performances both for club and country in the last two years have consistently been the best of his entire career.

With Paul Gascoigne (see page 127), Tony Adams is one of England's older heads. He is a natural leader at the back in a team full of captains, and the understanding between himself and his club teammate David Seaman (see page 247) in goal was crucial to the clean sheets that squeezed England above Italy in qualifying for France 98.

66 I thought to myself, 'that boy's going to play for England' when I first saw him aged 16. **99**
— *former England coach Bobby Robson*

DID YOU KNOW?
Adams has been an Arsenal player since 1983.

THIS PAGE: TONY ADAMS — WHEN HE WAS A TEENAGER, EXPERTS SAID HE'D BE ENGLAND'S CENTRE BACK FOR A DECADE. THEY WERE RIGHT.

OPPOSITE PAGE: THE STOPPER'S BALL SKILLS HAVE IMPROVED GREATLY OVER THE YEARS.

After his performances at USA 94, Aldair has become firmly recognized as being one of the best defenders in the game today. Brazil are perennially reckoned to be vulnerable at the back, where they are traditionally criticized for having a long history of disorganization and a string of weak goalkeepers. The facts do not bear this theory out. They conceded three goals in seven games at USA 94, when even the notoriously defensive beaten finalists Italy let in five on the way to the Final. If Brazil can field Aldair as they did at USA 94, when the now relative veteran of the Brazilian back-four took the place of Ricardo Rocha, they should have as solid a defence as any team.

This experienced stopper began his career at Flamengo in 1987. He played there for two seasons before moving to Lisbon, but the five goals he scored at Benfica had persuaded Roma to sign him after one season in Europe. In Italy he settled in quickly and well, winning a first-team place and keeping it. He now has eight years at Roma under his belt and is as regular in the club team as he is in his national side. Since becoming an international, he has missed only a handful of games for his country. His gangly figure will be the mainstay of the Brazilian defence at France 98. The only question is who will partner him at the back, as Andre Cruz is challenging Marcio Santos for the second shirt at the centre of Brazil's defence.

Fast, strong in the air and in the tackle, any team Aldair plays in can rely on a him for few goals over the season as well as the security of a defender who would challenge for a place in any more famously defensive team.

He is still often encouraged to come forward for set-pieces, where his height, positioning and timing can cause problems for goalkeepers.

FULL NAME:
Aldair Nascimento
dos Santos Aldair

BORN:
30.11.65

BIRTHPLACE:
Ilheus

HEIGHT:
1.87m/6ft 2in

WEIGHT:
77kg/12st 2lbs

CLUBS:
Flamengo, Benfica, Roma

DEBUT:
1988

HONOURS:
World Cup Winner 94, Copa
America winner 1989, 1997

66 **Aldair and Marcio Santos
will be called upon.** 99
— *national team coach
Mario Zagallo*

DID YOU KNOW?
Flamengo are reportedly interested
in re-signing Aldair.

THIS PAGE: ALDAIR — EXPERIENCE COUNTS
IN THE WORLD CUP, AND THEY DON'T COME
MORE EXPERIENCED THAN BRAZIL'S
MAINSTAY DEFENDER.

OPPOSITE PAGE: TAKING POSSESSION
AGAINST POLAND IN A FRIENDLY IN 1997.

DEFENCE
Argentina
AYALA

The unsung Roberto Ayala is probably Argentina's most reliable defender these days. His quiet contribution to the team effort belies the important role he plays in a defence that has had to go through some drastic changes since 1994. Ayala is one player who has slotted in well with the new arrangements. The simple efficiency of Argentina's passing football is often preceded by a timely intervention on the part of this young but mature stopper who has become part of the spine of the Argentine team. While experienced stalwarts like José Chamot have inexplicably faltered in the national side recently, Ayala's performances at the back of this workmanlike outfit have been consistently excellent throughout their successful qualification programme.

Ayala said he was 'proud' to be made captain of Napoli last season. It was an accolade the Italian club thought he thoroughly deserved, even if the responsibility was initially hard for him. The Naples captaincy carries a lot of history in Argentina; it was the title Diego Maradona (see page 12) had held in his time in the southern Italian city six years previously. Ayala was apparently reluctant to accept the captain's armband, but was eventually persuaded by the team's goalkeeper and former captain Giuseppe Tagliatela.

With compatriot Luis Calderon joining him at the Italian club from Independiente, it looks to some as if Naples are trying to regain their glory days by employing Argentinians again. If that is true, they've made a good start by selecting this reliable defender on whom to build another Championship challenging team. But although Naples are still in Serie A and reached the final of the Italian Cup in 1996, they still have a long way to go before they can hope to emulate their performances under Diego Maradona. The same is true for the Argentinian national team. A third World Cup Final in ten years may be too much to ask from this Argentine side, but with Ayala holding the line at the back, nobody will get the chance to accuse them of being suspect in defence.

> **❝** Throughout the history of Argentinian football, the people have only wanted to win. We players feel the same way. **❞**
> — *Roberto Ayala*

DID YOU KNOW?
Ayala has won the under-20 World Cup with Argentina.

THIS PAGE: ROBERTO AYALA — ARGENTINA'S NEW FACE CELEBRATES A GOAL IN THE PAN-AMERICAN CUP.

OPPOSITE PAGE: CONCENTRATION AND DETERMINATION ARE WHAT MAKE AYALA THE MAINSTAY OF SOUTH AMERICA'S BEST DEFENCE.

Norway
BERG

This versatile and reliable defender is a player who rarely allows an attacker to get the better of him. He is an extraordinarily shrewd reader of the game who always seems to be in the right place at the right time. He is also gifted with a crunching tackle that he times to perfection, and is always calm and collected, even under the greatest of pressure. But Henning Berg's greatest talent is that he tracks his man well and never commits to the tackle until the correct moment. Any amount of trickery will be to no avail as Norway's coolest customer stands up to his man and bides his time. Sooner or later, he knows that the attacker will try to go past him. That is when the Norwegian nonchalantly sticks out his right foot and relieves his adversary of the ball.

He cost big-spending Blackburn a mere £400,000 when he first went to England from Norway. One Premiership winner's medal later and his perceived value appreciated massively. So much so that Manchester United coach Alex Ferguson, who has rarely been known to shell out good money without reason, was prepared to break the bank to get his man. Concerned with England international Gary Pallister's recurrent back injury, and disappointed by his surprise failure to acquire a work permit for Brazilian international stopper Celio Silva, Ferguson showed no hesitation in paying neighbours Blackburn Rovers £5m for Henning Berg's services at the beginning of last season.

Although he was a right-back in Blackburn's English Premiership-winning team of 1995, he usually plays at centre-back for his country. This is also the role he normally assumes for Manchester United, when selected, but he has always looked equally comfortable playing at full-back on either side of the defence. With Manchester United teammate Ronny Johnsen, as well as fellow Premiership stars Gunnar Halle (see page 186) and Alf Inge Haaland all fit, Berg may be expected to play out wide on the left in France. But wherever he plays, his solid, no-nonsense style of football will add further strength to an already formidable looking team whose tight defence was their greatest strength in the qualifying programme.

FULL NAME:
Henning Berg

BORN:
1.9.69

BIRTHPLACE:
Eidsvoll

HEIGHT:
1.80m/5ft 11in

WEIGHT:
79kg/12st 6lbs

CLUBS:
Lillestrom, Blackburn Rovers, Manchester United

DEBUT:
1992

> 66 We don't play nice pretty football, but we've changed a bit. We don't knock long ball all the time now. 99
> — *Henning Berg on Norway's football style*

DID YOU KNOW?
Henning Berg was voted Norwegian Player of the Year in 1995.

THIS PAGE: HENNING BERG — BACK ON FORM FOR BLACKBURN AND NORWAY, WHO MUST FANCY THEIR CHANCES OF WINNING THE WORLD CUP FOR THE FIRST TIME EVER.

OPPOSITE PAGE: HENNING BERG MAKES ANOTHER PERFECTLY TIMED CHALLENGE.

FULL NAME:
Roberto Carlos

BORN:
10.04.73

BITHPLACE:
Garca, São Paolo

HEIGHT:
1.68m/5ft 6in

WEIGHT:
69kg/10st 12lbs

CLUBS:
Uniao São Joao, Palmeiras,
São Paolo, Inter Milan,
Real Madrid

DEBUT:
1991

INTERNATIONAL HONOURS:
Copa America winner 1997

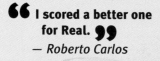

**I scored a better one
for Real.**
— *Roberto Carlos*

DID YOU KNOW?
Real Madrid had first watched him
playing for Palmeiras but
considered him too short to make
a top full-back.

THIS PAGE: ROBERTO CARLOS — GOOD
ENOUGH TO MAKE HIS NAME IN FRANCE
AS THE WORLD'S GREATEST LEFT BACK.

OPPOSITE PAGE: PREPARING TO BELT THE
BALL WITH HIS TRUSTY LEFT FOOT.

Perhaps this attacking left-back is best known for smiling. And for the 42-yard wickedly twisting free-kick he scored against France in Le Tournoi; the ball went so far over to the right before slicing left and correcting itself for the back of the net that it even sent the ballboy the wrong way. Brazilians will also remember the 35-yarder he scored against Gremio in 1995. A lot of defenders have shuddered in the wall since the days when this man's biggest claim to fame was that he was the namesake of a top Brazilian crooner.

From the time of his international debut as an 18-year-old, he became a regular under Carlos Alberto Parreira, even though he stayed in his home province of São Paolo until the end of 1992. He then spent two and a half years at Palmeiras at a time when they were universally recognised as the best side in Brazil. By the time he left for Italy, his £5m transfer fee was the biggest ever involving a Brazilian club. He had nevertheless been dropped for the USA 94 qualifiers, and didn't get anywhere near the Finals. Indeed, he spent nearly two years without winning a cap before being selected again for a friendly against Israel. Since then, he has proved his international credentials once again with impressive performances in the Umbro Cup, including a goal against Japan.

He joined Real Madrid from Inter Milan, as he puts it: 'as a result of the Bosman ruling and the fact that Inter had signed too many foreigners'. He is now contracted to the Spanish club until 2002 and was an ever-present in the victorious Copa America 1997 team.

The man with the tree-trunk legs he says he inherited from his father is now definitely back as an automatic first choice for Brazil. Datafolha, a Brazilian organization specialising in match statistics, calculated that in his last São Paolo Championship, he averaged 3.6 shots per game, more than any other player. They also reckoned he had set up a teammate for a goalscoring opportunity at a rate of one per game. Teams at France 98 will also be trying to avoid giving away free-kicks within 40 yards of their goal.

Holland
DE BOER

FULL NAME:
Frank de Boer

BORN:
15.5.70

BIRTHPLACE:
Hoorn

HEIGHT:
1.79m/5ft 10in

WEIGHT:
79kg/12st 6lbs

CLUBS:
Ajax

DEBUT:
1990

❝I have always been happy at Ajax. ❞
— *Frank de Boer*

DID YOU KNOW?
At Ajax, Frank de Boer is still known to stay behind after training and practise his dead-ball skills over and over again.

THIS PAGE: FRANK DE BOER — THE MAN IN CONTROL OF THE DUTCH DEFENCE FOR THE LAST EIGHT YEARS IS COMING INTO HIS PRIME.

OPPOSITE PAGE: HOLLAND'S ABILITY IN ATTACK IS UNDISPUTED. FRANK DE BOER IS THE UNSUNG HERO IN DEFENCE.

Holland's first choice central defender made his Ajax debut way back in 1988. His contribution to that 4–1 win over PEC Zwolle was the start of an uninterrupted ten-year career at the club where he plays with his twin brother Ronald (see page 117). Now Sjaak Swart's all-time record of 463 matches for the Amsterdam club looks in extreme danger. Frank de Boer has another 200 games to go before he breaks that record and becomes 'Mr Ajax', but he signed a contract at the beginning of this season to stay at the Amsterdam club for a further six years. During this time, he is also likely to win a century of caps for Holland.

Frank, who is slightly the smaller of the two twins, made his international debut just after Italia 90 in a friendly against the Italians in Palermo. The Dutch lost 1–0 that day but Frank de Boer kept his place to become the mainstay of the Dutch defence in the 1990s and the ideal replacement for Ronald Koeman. He should collect his 50th international cap in France and is likely to stay in the national team for the next World Cup at least.

More than Koeman, he is a defender who likes to get forward. Sometimes he takes the Dutch fans' war-cry of 'Aanvallen! Aanvallen!' (Attack! Attack!) a little too literally, worrying the life out of his teammates as he seeks his own moment of glory. However, his undoubted skill as a dead-ball specialist combined with his powerful header are enough to calm his colleagues' worries. Frank de Boer is also known both at club and international level for his expertise with free-kicks.

That he missed Euro 96 with an ankle injury will be no excuse for coaches to forget how central this player has been at the back of the Dutch. Frank de Boer played at USA 94 and was invaluable to the Dutch team on their progress to the quarter-finals. His defensive experience and sharp shooting skills were sorely missed at Euro 96, where many people's pre-tournament favourites failed to impress. He will be hoping to make amends in 1998.

France
DESAILLY

Marcel Desailly is the mainstay of any defence he plays in. In fact, it surprises many French people that this versatile and powerful player has not collected as many caps as they believe his talents merit.

He made a name for himself during his six-year stint at Nantes after coming to France from his birthplace in Ghana. Then he signed for Marseille where he believed that he had then reached the pinnacle of his career. He was playing for what was then easily the best team in France and, in his final year there, the best team in all of Europe – a claim they proved by winning the European Cup. But although this distinctive figure claims never to have thought of leaving France, his contribution to Marseille's success had been well noted, and AC Milan stepped in to snap him up. Desailly admitted then that the move to a club with such a famous history was awe-inspiring. Despite this, he settled in quickly and well, immediately claiming a regular first-team place and helping his new club to win two Italian League Championships.

Although he usually plays in the centre of midfield at club level, he has expressed a preference to play at the back for the national team, a position in which he is equally outstanding. He can also play right-back at a pinch, and given that this is not a position in which his country's international squad is over-endowed, he may switch to there during the course of France 98.

Now, having proved himself at the highest club level in both France and Italy, there seems little reason to believe that the man they call 'the rock' will not be the foundation upon which the French defence is built. And you can be sure that there won't be many attackers who relish the thought of playing against the big man.

FULL NAME:
Marcel Desailly
BORN:
7.9.68
BIRTHPLACE:
Accra, Ghana
HEIGHT:
1.85m/6ft 1in
WEIGHT:
85kg/13st 6lbs
CLUBS:
Nantes, Marseille, AC Milan
DEBUT:
1993

❝ You're doing us good defensively. ❞
— *Milan teammate and legendary defender Franco Baresi*
(see page 168)

DID YOU KNOW?
Desailly has won successive European Cups: with Marseille in 1993 and Milan in 1994.

THIS PAGE: MARCEL DESAILLY – 'THE ROCK' IS THE FOUNDATION OF THIS STEADY FRENCH DEFENCE AND ONE OF THE BEST IN THE WORLD.

OPPOSITE PAGE: COMING OUT OF DEFENCE WITH THE BALL.

South Africa
FISH

The young star of South Africa is unmistakable. He's the loping, facially expressive white boy at the back whose ungainly and unkempt appearance disguise what is potentially the best all-round talent South Africa have. Despite his youth, he has experience of Serie A, the English Premiership and has played over 30 times for the 'Bafana Bafana' as South Africa are known at home. Indeed, national coach Clive Barker once said Fish was his first, second and third choice in the national team. He is a hero to the fans, an inspiration to those playing around him, he reads attacks well and marshals the defence accordingly, and he is a persistent tackler.

While he was playing in South Africa, Fish had a reputation as a lively socializer as well. Ex-Pirates teammate Edward Motale once recalled of their trips into Pretoria: 'Fish is not like other whites. I take him to Mamelodi, to Tembisa, and he'll get up and dance, even though he's the only white. He won't give a damn, he'll just boogie, and then others will join him.' Fish has the advantage that he is too young to fully remember Apartheid and the Soweto uprising. This has made it easier for him to cross the 'railway' between black and white South Africa.

He has proved himself as a player in Europe but is still criticized for following the ball upfield and playing as a striker. This is very much a part of his game, however, and the short-lived spectacle of the World Cup, where one moment of genius can make you a legend, is the place for him to exercize it. Some would say this temptation to join the attack extends to the entire South African squad and that their inexperience at World Cup level will let them down. But the *Bafana Bafana* are African Champions and, as long as they have potential match-winners like 'the Feesh', they will be a threat to any team.

FULL NAME:
Mark Fish

BORN:
14.3.74

BIRTHPLACE:
Cape Town

HEIGHT:
1.92m/6ft 3in

WEIGHT:
84kg/13st 3lbs

CLUBS:
Arcadia Shepherds, Jomo Cosmos, Orlando Pirates, Lazio, Bolton Wanderers

DEBUT:
1993

INTERNATIONAL HONOURS:
African Nations Cup winner 1996

❝ What impresses most people about Mark Fish is his body language. He betrays to the crowds what we're trying to get across. ❞
— *national coach Clive Barker*

DID YOU KNOW?
Orlando Pirates fans would take fresh fish to matches and wave them to the chant of 'Feesh!' whenever their hero touched the ball.

THIS PAGE: MARK FISH — APPARENTLY WOMEN FIND HIM ATTRACTIVE. THE APPEAL MUST BE IN HIS FOOTBALLING SKILLS.

OPPOSITE PAGE: JUMPING TO TAKE THE BALL AGAINST ENGLAND IN A FRIENDLY LAST YEAR.

Full name:
Gunnar Halle

Born:
11.8.65

Birthplace:
Oslo

Height:
1.82m/5ft 11in

Weight:
71kg/11st 2lbs

Clubs:
Lillestrom, Oldham Athletic, Leeds United

Debut:
1987

A utility player who is one of the unsung heroes of the English Premiership, Gunnar Halle has been playing his football in England since February 1991, when he signed for Oldham at a cost of £300,000. His skills were put to best use on the right side of midfield during his five seasons there. However, he looked comfortable playing anywhere in defence, or even as a defensive midfielder in the anchor position just in front of the back line where his great positional sense cuts the amount of running he had to do. But if he has to run, he can do so all day. He has incredible stamina, is very quick and is also a much better passer of the ball than most people give him credit for.

Gunnar Halle transferred to Leeds in December 1996 for a bargain £400,000 after coach George Graham had failed to sign John Scales from Liverpool. Scales' preference for Tottenham Hotspur was a disappointment to Leeds fans at the time, but Gunnar Halle has been a more than adequate alternative. The added bonus was that he cost the Yorkshire club a tenth of the fee that the former Liverpool defender would have commanded. In his time at Leeds, Halle has most often been employed at right-back with his international teammate Alf Inge Haaland playing in a central role, although he has also played in the middle of a three-man defence.

Halle's introduction to Elland Road was far from easy. The club was in turmoil when he arrived and lost three successive League games over the Christmas period after he signed. But the Norwegian proved himself in the fourth round of the FA Cup at Arsenal as Leeds successfully defended an early lead given them by a Rodney Wallace goal. He has since become a regular fixture in George Graham's parsimonious Leeds defence.

He has collected over 60 caps for his country and his influence on the team has been key to its impressive FIFA ranking. Norway may not have the finesse or the personnel to challenge for the trophy, but nobody will relish the prospect of facing the hard-working Norwegians in France.

> 66 **The only place Gunnar Halle hasn't played for the Norwegian national team is centre-forward or goalkeeper.** 99
> — *Nils Johan Samb, Norwegian coach after France 98*

DID YOU KNOW?
Gunnar Halle expressed a desire to return to Norway at the start of last season, but remains at Leeds.

THIS PAGE: GUNNAR HALLE — THE NORWEGIAN COLLECTS HIS THOUGHTS BEFORE PLAYING IN THE 4–0 DEMOLITION OF FINLAND IN QUALIFYING.

OPPOSITE PAGE: GETS FORWARD DOWN THE WING AND LOOKS UP TO MAKE THE CROSS.

Scotland
HENDRY

Given his current form for both club and country, it is astonishing to remember that Colin Hendry didn't make it into the international set up until the age of 28. As an international footballer, he was a late starter whose weaknesses in defence caused him to be considered too unreliable for the game at the highest level. But although he took a long time to come to prominence for Scotland, the big centre-back with the long blond hair is one of the world's most determined stoppers. The Scottish defence would now look a lot more vulnerable without his dominating presence.

As well as his marshalling of the defence, Colin Hendry is a player who enjoys getting forward. In two spells at Blackburn, he has averaged a goal every ten games in well over 300 first team appearances, not a bad tally for a central defender. Despite this record however, this tendency to push forward was often criticized earlier in his career when he too frequently left his teammates vulnerable to counter-attacks during these forays into his opponents' half. But under the guidance of former club coach and compatriot Kenny Dalglish, his wanderings were curtailed at Blackburn and Hendry quickly began to develop into the top class defender that he is today.

In helping Dalglish's Blackburn Rovers to their first English League win in 81 years, Hendry showed unerring control of his own penalty area and the spirit of a man who never doubted his team's ability to prove themselves the best in England in 1995. His subsequent performances in Scotland's tour of Japan that summer earned him a regular spot at the back for his country that he has never since looked like relinquishing. Since that famous win, Blackburn have never again lived up to those levels, but under new club coach Roy Hodgson, Colin Hendry is now getting back to something approaching that Championship form. It is no coincidence that Blackburn's fortunes took a similar upturn last season. In the early part of last season, Hendry's club coach told his national coach that the form of this most important defender had been 'immense' since returning from injury. Craig Brown has since been given no reason to doubt that judgement.

FULL NAME:
Edward Colin James Hendry

BORN:
7.12.65

BIRTHPLACE:
Keith

HEIGHT:
1.86m/6ft 1in

WEIGHT:
76kg /12st

CLUBS:
Dundee, Manchester City, Blackburn Rovers

DEBUT:
1993

> 66 Colin Hendry is outstanding. He's the first pick. 99
> — *national coach Craig Brown*

DID YOU KNOW?
Craig Brown rates Colin's seven year old son Kyle as an 'unbelievable' player.

THIS PAGE: COLIN HENDRY — IF HE CAN SHUT OUT THE OPPOSITION, SCOTLAND SHOULD BE ON THEIR WAY TO THEIR BEST EVER WORLD CUP PERFORMANCE.

OPPOSITE PAGE: SCOTLAND'S MAINSTAY AT THE BACK KEEPS ANOTHER CLEAN SHEET AGAINST SWEDEN IN QUALIFYING.

FULL NAME:
Masami Ihara

BORN:
18.9.67

BIRTHPLACE:
Shiga

HEIGHT:
1.82m/6ft

WEIGHT:
72kg/11st 5lbs

CLUBS:
Tsukuba University,
Yokohama Marinos

DEBUT:
1988

INTERNATIONAL HONOURS:
Asian Cup winner 1992

66 We want to know, if we get the Cup, can we make it to the next level? **99**
— *Masami Ihara just before Japan was given the 2002 World Cup*

DID YOU KNOW?
Ihara has been a Marinos player since 1992 and has played in the J-League throughout its short history.

THIS PAGE: MASAMI IHARA — THE VETERAN'S INFLUENCE CAN HELP THE JAPANESE PULL OFF A SHOCK ON THEIR WORLD CUP DEBUT.

OPPOSITE PAGE: EQUALLY COMPETENT BOTH AS A SWEEPER AND AS A MARKER, IHARA GIVES THE TEAM VERSATILITY AND POISE.

Veteran goalscoring star Kazu Miura and the Brazilian-born new recruit Wagner Lopez may catch the eye as Japan's attacking partnership in France, but Asia's most improved team continues to revolve around its captain and most dependable defender, Masimi Ihara.

Ihara usually plays in the middle of a flat back-four, but he is more than competent as a sweeper whenever his team moves to a more attacking 3–5–2 formation. He has been a regular at the back since he was a university student, and it is no coincidence that his 100 caps have coincided with Japan's climb to a previously undreamed of Top 20 FIFA ranking. The Japanese have yet to prove themselves as a world force in competitive international football, but under Ihara's captaincy, they will now at least have the experience of World Cup football this summer to prepare them for the World Cup they will host in 2002.

Had they not made it to France, the Japanese would have won the dubious distinction of becoming the first World Cup hosts never to have qualified for a finals series in their own right. But the only surprise in their qualification this time was the hard work they made of it. The overall form of Ihara's team has improved greatly since heavy defeats to France in 1994, and to Nigeria and Argentina in 1995. The captain has since led his team to a 4–3 defeat of Croatia a couple of years ago, as well as a less remarkable, but equally difficult, 1–0 away win over Tunisia, despite Ihara becoming 'exhausted, because it was so hot'.

Coach Shu Kamo knows that he has the youngster Saitou on the bench, but that is just in case. The Shimizu S-Pulse player replaced Ihara for the game against Romania in the King's Cup in Bangkok recently, apparently to good effect, but Saitou's only hope of a finals appearance this time round will be as Ihara's defensive partner. Japan will need their captain in order to make a good impression in France, probably more than they will need any of their more high-profile attacking stars.

DEFENCE
Bulgaria
IVANOV

Trifon Ivanov is the captain and defensive mainstay of one of the most exciting and successful teams in international football at the moment. Semi-finalists at USA 94, his team has again come through a tough qualifying group that included Russia and a greatly improved Israel with ease. Upon qualifying for France, coach Hristo Bonev announced that his squad would 'get ready calmly so that we can correct our mistakes and present Bulgarian football in France with dignity'. His captain doesn't make very many mistakes at the back, and he is dignity personified.

Ivanov's career has taken him from Sofia to Spain and Switzerland, and he has now won the Austrian Bundesliga and played in the final of the European Cup Winners' Cup with Rapid Vienna. He is a tenacious defender who has the distinct look of a man who is always fully concentrated on the game in hand. He times his tackles accurately and shows great skill and composure on the ball. He will be seen guarding his goalkeeper's post to defend against opposition set-pieces, and he is also well known for the blistering shot which he uses as a simple but effective strategy for long range free-kicks. But the Bulgarian team looks best when they're pressurizing their opponents with sweeping passing moves that allow players from the back to get up into the box. Ivanov is one of the keenest to get forward and join the attack. He is always a likely source of goals.

Given the high regard in which the Bulgarians have been held ever since the last World Cup, and taking into account their impressive performance in qualifying for France at the expense of a team with a top ten FIFA ranking, it is astonishing to remember that before 1994, Ivanov's team had never won a match at a World Cup finals in five appearances. But with skipper Ivanov at the back, as well as Stoichkov (see page 82) and Letchkov (see page 140) still playing, the spine of the 1994 semi-finalists is still intact. On their day, they can beat anybody.

FULL NAME:
Trifon Marinov Ivanov

BORN:
27.7.65

BIRTHPLACE:
Lpinitiza

HEIGHT:
1.81m/5ft 11in

WEIGHT:
71kg/11st 2lbs

CLUBS:
Etar, CSKA, Real Betis, Xamax Neuchatel, Rapid Vienna

DEBUT:
1987

> **❝ I am happy that our generation of footballers is qualifying for the World Cup finals for a second time. ❞**
> *— Trifon Ivanov*

DID YOU KNOW?
Ivanov scored the captain's goal against qualifying group rivals Russia in Sofia that guaranteed his country a place at France 98.

THIS PAGE: TRIFON IVANOV — JUST THE LOOK OF HIM STRIKES FEAR INTO OPPOSITION ATTACKERS.

OPPOSITE PAGE: THE MAINSTAY OF THE BULGARIAN DEFENCE FOR OVER A DECADE.

Germany
KOHLER

FULL NAME:
Jürgen Kohler

BORN:
6.10.65

BIRTHPLACE:
Lambsheim

HEIGHT:
1.86m/6ft 1in

WEIGHT:
85kg/13st 5lbs

CLUBS:
Bayern Munich, Juventus,
Borussia Dortmund

DEBUT:
1988

INTERNATIONAL HONOURS:
World Cup winner 1990,
European Championships
winner 1996

66 I don't like easy rides. The
tougher the game, the better
I like it. **99**
— *Jürgen Kohler*

DID YOU KNOW?
Kohler's nickname in Germany
is 'Iron Foot'

THIS PAGE: JÜRGEN KOHLER — A REGULAR
FIXTURE IN GERMANY'S EVER-EFFICIENT
DEFENCE.

OPPOSITE PAGE: TAKING THE BALL AWAY
FROM A DANISH PLAYER IN A RECENT
2–0 VICTORY.

Germany's best stopper for the last ten years went out of Euro 96 with torn knee ligaments sustained in the first game and missed the rest of the tournament. You may not see a lot of Jürgen Kohler at France 98 either. There's little doubt that he'll be playing on the right side of a three-man defence in a team that, as always, has every chance of going all the way to the final, but he goes about his work quietly. A deft touch here and a convincing header there is usually enough. Then he jogs silently backwards to take up his position on the edge of the penalty area and is not seen until the opposition dares to disturb him again. With Germany on the ball, this can be some time.

When he returned from Italy, he was considered to be nearing the end of his usefulness, but Dortmund have now won Europe's most coveted club trophy with him at the back. Kohler is on the top of his form again this season and recntly said: 'I would like to think it's still possible to take part in some more big wins before I eventually retire.' He was instrumental in Dortmund's European Champions League Cup victory in 1997 when he saved the day at Old Trafford by blocking an Eric Cantona shot in the semi-final against Manchester United. His dependability at the back then overcame all the efforts of his former Juve teammates in the final as well as earning him the German player of the year award.

He never lets his concentration slip. When involved in close marking he can follow his man step for step, never giving him any room for any World Cup chicanery. Kohler is always playing for the good of the team and his contribution to their success is significant. As his club coach Nevio Scala says, 'players like him are a catalyst. Their pride and appetite for victory encourages others in the team to raise their game.'

With his bright red hair and ginger goatee, Alexei Lalas was the first name we all learned from that team of unknowns who represented the host nation at the 1994 World Cup Finals. But it wasn't just for his appearance. Lalas was as solid as a rock in the USA defence and always looked dangerous whenever he came forward for a set piece.

England had previously learned about him the hard way when the centre-back leaped above their defence to score in a 2–0 victory in 1993. It was an unexpected goal in an unexpected result, but the Haitians could have warned England coach Graham Taylor about Lalas before then. He had scored twice against them in an 8–1 defeat on the road to the 1992 Olympics.

He's up towards a century of caps now, although he was surprisingly left out of coach Steve Sampson's USA team for a qualifier against Costa Rica last year. Until then, he had been an ever-present for the USA for four years, scoring a total of nine goals; not bad for a defender. He played every minute of the USA's 1994 campaign, and has since represented his country in the Copa America and the Olympic Games. His showing in 1994 earned him a contract with Italian club Padova, newly promoted to Serie A. There he set two firsts: he was the first ever United States citizen to play in Serie A, and he started his career in Italy by scoring his club's first ever goal in the top flight, a headed winner over the mighty AC Milan.

Despite expressing his amazement at the continued success of his career in football, Lalas has been constantly showered with accolades for his sporting prowess since high school. He has now collected vast banks of football experience to draw from, and the fact that he has now become known to the entire world is sometimes enough to ensure the presence of this powerful and vital player in either penalty area.

FULL NAME:
Alexei Lalas

BORN:
1.6.70

BIRTHPLACE:
Birmingham, MI

HEIGHT:
1.89m/6ft 2in

WEIGHT:
88kg/ 13st 12lbs

CLUBS:
Padova, New England Revolution

DEBUT:
1993

❝ I never once thought I could be an athlete and make a career from that. ❞
— *Alexei Lalas*

DID YOU KNOW?
Lalas once captained his high school team to the state ice hockey title.

THIS PAGE: ALEXEI LALAS — THE MAN WHO WANTED TO BE A ROCK STAR SETTLES FOR INTERNATIONAL FOOTBALL STARDOM IN THE 1995 COPA AMERICA.

OPPOSITE PAGE: LALAS BATTLES FOR THE BALL AGAINST TRINIDAD AND TOBAGO IN THE 1996 CONACAF GOLD CUP.

Italy
MALDINI

FULL NAME:
Paolo Maldini

BORN:
26.6.68

BIRTHPLACE:
Milano

HEIGHT:
1.85m/6ft 1in

WEIGHT:
68kg/10st 10lbs

CLUBS:
AC Milan

DEBUT:
1988

The best left-back in the world is now trying to prove himself as the best sweeper in the world. Whether his performances in that position in France will win him that acclaim remains to be seen, but in 1995, Morocco's French coach Henri Michel considered Maldini to be the best player in the world in any position.

With his father Cesare coaching him from the sidelines, Paolo Maldini looks the perfect captain. 'I have been very proud of the way Paolo has conducted himself as a footballer,' says the coach. 'People may think I say this because I am his father, but I believe that no-one with an objective mind can fault my analysis.'

AC Milan's local lad is a one-club man. He made his first League appearance for AC Milan in 1985 at the age of just 16 and was so impressive that he became the team's regular left-back the following season. That same year, he was also selected for the Italian under-21s where he scored five goals in 12 games. He won his first full cap on the last day of March 1988 and is now approaching his 100th game for Italy.

When Franco Baresi (see page 168) retired, Maldini was asked to fill his boots as the defensive organizer for both Milan and Italy. His reading of the game and leadership qualities made him the obvious candidate from within the Milan set-up at that time. But Maldini took time to adapt to filling the gap that the former national team captain's retirement had left. Milan fell to a mid-table mediocrity from which they have yet to recover, while Italy qualified for France the hard way, coming up against an improving England in their qualifying group and the ever-capable Russians in the play-offs. Given the circumstances, it is a credit to both father and son that the Italians will be making their customary appearance at the World Cup Finals, and against both England and Russia in the final three qualifying games, young Paolo looked like he was starting to get the hang of it all.

> **" Figlio d'arte (bred for the job). "**
> — *Italian football pundit Paddy Agnew*

DID YOU KNOW?
Maldini's father won 14 caps and the European Cup as Italy and AC Milan's sweeper in the early 1960s.

THIS PAGE: PAOLO MALDINI — THE WORLD'S GREATEST LEFT-BACK HOPES TO BECOME RECOGNIZED AS THE WORLD'S GREATEST SWEEPER.

OPPOSITE PAGE: THE FATHER-AND-SON PARTNERSHIP COULD WELL LIFT THE TROPHY IN JULY.

Yugoslavia
MIHAJLOVIC

One of the most accomplished centre-halves in Serie A, Sinisa Mihajlovic is employed as a sweeper by national-team boss Slobadon Santrac. This position suits his natural game as it permits him to combine his defensive duties with his undoubted skill at bringing the ball out of defence to initiate attacking moves.

Another member of the European Cup-winning Red Star Belgrade side of 1991, Mihajlovic was signed by his countryman Vujadin Boskov for Roma in September 1992. The £3.5m man enjoyed two seasons in the Italian capital before transferring to Sampdoria, where his football always seemed to continue to improve with the experience he was gaining in the Italian league.

But after the high praise he received over the course of the 1996/97 season, the beginning of the new season proved rather more difficult for the 29-year-old at club level. Apparently unhappy with the style of Sampdoria's new Argentinian coach, Cesar Menotti, and serving several lengthy bans for a spate of red and yellow cards, Mihajlovic seemed to be saving his best performances for Yugoslavia's World Cup qualifiers. There he was the fulcrum of a defence that conceded only seven goals in ten matches. But Menotti's resignation from Sampdoria last November, and the subsequent arrival of Mihajlovic's old Roma boss in his place has brought a new upturn in form for the Yugoslav.

Having been deprived of international football for two and a half years when the United Nations imposed sanctions on Serbia and Montenegro, the civil war in his homeland effectively cost Mihajlovic his chance to participate in the last two European Championships as well as the 1994 World Cup. 'A career as a professional footballer is pretty short, so it was very frustrating for our national team to be frozen out for a long time,' he admits. 'It's hard when you see your clubmates called up for internationals and you are left at home.' But this summer, Mihajlovic will finally have the opportunity he deserves, to test himself against the best strikers the World Cup has to offer.

FULL NAME:
Sinisa Mihajlovic
BORN:
20.2.69
BIRTHPLACE:
Vukovar
HEIGHT:
1.85m/6ft 1in
WEIGHT:
78kg/12st 4lbs
CLUBS:
Vojvodina, Red Star Belgrade, Roma, Sampdoria
DEBUT:
1990

> **So many of us have never played in a major international competition, so we desperately want to succeed in France.**
> — Sinisa Mihajlovic

DID YOU KNOW?
When the 1995 Cup-Winners Cup semi-final between Sampdoria and Arsenal finished 5–5 on aggregate, Mihajlovic took the first kick of the penalty shoot-out and had it saved by David Seaman (see page 247).

THIS PAGE: SINISA MIHAJLOVIC — THIS VERSATILE AND RELIABLE DEFENDER WILL FINALLY GET THE CHANCE TO PROVE HIMSELF ON THE BIGGEST STAGE.

OPPOSITE PAGE: YUGOSLAVS WILL HOPE MIHAJLOVIC KEEPS OUT OF THE REFEREE'S NOTEBOOK IN FRANCE.

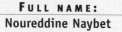

Morocco
NAYBET

FULL NAME:
Noureddine Naybet

BORN:
10.2.70

BIRTHPLACE:
Casablanca

HEIGHT:
1.82m/6ft

WEIGHT:
75 kg/12st

CLUBS:
Raja Casablanca, Nantes,
Sporting Lisbon,
Deportivo La Coruña

O ne of the best defenders playing today is this vastly experienced star of the Moroccan team. Naybet is an uncompromizing tackler who times his challenges perfectly and often comes out with the ball at his feet. But he is not a dirty player, and his disciplinary record is a testament to his character on the field. Although he often finds himself as the last line of defence, he very rarely gets booked, preferring to use his positional sense to thwart attackers rather than resorting to bringing them down. But despite his unquestioned abilities as a man-marker, Naybet is more usually employed as a sweeper. His distribution is excellent and many a Moroccan counter-attack begins with a sweeping cross-field pass from the *libero*. He is also a player who takes the opportunity to go forward whenever it arises. He can shoot as well as most strikers and his heading ability is often employed at set pieces.

Naybet appeared at the last World Cup, but the world did not see him at his best. Since then, though, his club career has developed well and the three-time winner of the Moroccan League has now won his first major European trophy, the Portuguese Cup, with Sporting Lisbon.

In the summer of 1996 Naybet went north to Deportivo for a bargain price of a little over £1m. That club's recent rise in fortunes has largely been made on the back of a tight defence, and the inclusion of the Moroccan in their ranks has only served to strengthen them in that department. In 1997, Deportivo conceded fewer goals than any other team in the Spanish League, a meagre 30 in 42 League matches. Their new recruit was a major contributing factor in that record and the Galicians look like keeping Naybet at the heart of their defence for the foreseeable future. He is contracted to Deportivo until the year 2000, and although his £1m get-out clause is nothing compared to that of the Brazilian Djalminha (see page 123), he is just as important to his club side as the South American and he is essential to the national team.

> **❝ Naybet appeared at the last World Cup, but the world did not see him at his best. ❞**

DID YOU KNOW?
Morocco's last goal in the qualifying rounds was academic for scorer Naybet. They had already booked their trip to France with two games in hand.

THIS PAGE: NOUREDDINE NAYBET — CAPTAIN AND STAR OF THE UNDER-RATED AFRICANS.

OPPOSITE PAGE: NAYBET IS RESPONSIBLE FOR KEEPING THE SHAPE OF THE TEAM — HE IS MOROCCO'S 'MANAGER ON THE PITCH'.

Nigeria
OLISEH

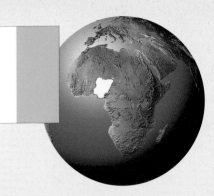

The Ajax all-rounder is a relative newcomer to the squad but he has been around long enough to have earned a reputation in Nigeria as one of their greatest prospects. He plays in midfield, usually on the left-side of a free-wheeling 4–3–3. Like so many of his teammates, he is combative in defence and collected in possession, but the quality of Oliseh's first touch gives him a little bit of extra time to pick out his best option. He is a player who is often found in the middle of a dangerous move, quietly probing the opposition's defences for weaknesses. He often changes position over the course of a match, and if Nigeria ever revert to the 3–5–2 they were playing before their African Nations Cup success, Oliseh might be pushed out to play as a left wing-back, a position he has coped with well at Ajax.

As a Bundesliga champion with Köln, he moved to Holland last summer. The fluidity of the Ajax system is similar to that used by the Nigerians these days, and Oliseh fits well into both styles of play. He is a natural footballer who seems equally at ease in almost any position. A highly reliable passer of the ball, he tracks back and tackles with boundless enthusiasm and is quite capable of converting any chances that come his way. Ajax fans were given an immediate demonstration of this important facet of his game at the beginning of last season, when he scored on his League debut in the 5–0 thrashing of Vitesse. He later opened his European account in the 9–0 first round UEFA Cup devastation of Slovenian club Maribor.

He is still only 23, but Oliseh is another Nigerian who has the experiences of USA 94 to draw from, and was also one of the stars of the Olympic Games victory. He may not yet be at his peak, but if Nigeria can keep possession of the ball, he will be instrumental in their build-up and may well finish on the end of the final ball.

FULL NAME:
Ogorchukwu Sunday Oliseh

BORN:
14.09.74

BIRTHPLACE:
Abavo

HEIGHT:
1.83m/6ft

WEIGHT:
78kg/12st 4lbs

CLUBS:
Julius Berger, Liege, Reggiana, Köln, Ajax

INTERNATIONAL HONOURS:
African Nations Cup winner 1994

66 The best African player at the 1994 World Cup finals. **99**
— *George Weah, Liberian international and former European and African Player of the Year*

DID YOU KNOW?
Oliseh scored the opening goal in the 3–0 defeat of Kenya that booked Nigeria their second consecutive World Cup place.

THIS PAGE: SUNDAY OLISEH — CONTINUING THE RECENT TRADITION OF GREAT NIGERIAN FOOTBALL PLAYERS.

OPPOSITE PAGE: THE LATEST NIGERIAN TO MAKE A NAME FOR HIMSELF IN EUROPE.

DEFENCE
Paraguay
'GAMARRA' PAVON

FULL NAME:
Carlos Alberto Gamarra Pavon

BORN:
17.2.71

BIRTHPLACE:
Asuncion

HEIGHT:
1.86m/6ft 1in

WEIGHT:
80kg/12st 8lbs

CLUBS:
30 de Agosto, Capiatenya,
Internacional de Porto Alegre,
Benfica

DEBUT:
1992

66 With this defence, we have a team that can challenge for the World Cup title. **99**
— *Carlos Gamarra Pavon*

DID YOU KNOW?
Gamarra came forward to score a total of three goals in qualification, all of them in 2–1 victories in Asuncion.

THIS PAGE: CARLOS ALBERTO GAMARRA — THE FIRST LINE OF ATTACK.

OPPOSITE PAGE: GAMARRA'S TEAM LOOK AS STRONG AS ANY OF THE OTHER CONTENDERS IN THE FIRST ROUND'S 'GROUP OF DEATH'.

Put simply, Gamarra is the man in the middle at the back. Under Brazilian coach Paulo Cesar Carpegiani, Paraguay tend to play with a sweeper, two centre-backs, and two lateral players who push up to support the midfield. The team likes to pack the middle of the park and plays most of its best football there. The Paraguayans are capable of keeping the ball for long periods of time with short, accurate passes that seek to penetrate weaknesses in the opposition's defence. Gamarra is the source of many of their better moves and is always on hand to take the ball back from the midfielders whenever his teammates come under pressure in possession.

As well as orchestrating the attack from the back line, Gamarra has all the qualities of a top class defender. He is a quick and intelligent player whose power in the air makes it very difficult for opponents to get any joy from hopeful long balls into the box. Gamarra can stand on the edge of the penalty area all day, cleaning up the loose balls and playing them out to his wing-backs or heading the ball out to touch if he has to. He is a player who never takes risks, and thrives on his ability to do the simple things well. With Gamarra at the back, Paraguay ensured their qualification by having the tightest defence in the South American qualifying group.

The sweeper has an eye for goal too, as he showed in qualification against Colombia, getting onto the end of a Francisco Arce cross to give his team a sixth-minute lead in their vital 2–1 victory in Los Defensores del Chaco, the national stadium in Asuncion.

Playing in Brazil for Internacional last summer, Carlos Gamarra came under pressure from his club to miss his country's trip to the United States until FIFA intervened on behalf of the 'Guaranies' (Paraguayans). Coach Carpegiani had already named a 22-man squad without Gamarra in it, but he had also left a place for his most important defender, should he be able to travel with the party. Gamarra is that important to Paraguay.

Nominally an attacking right-sided wing-back, Dan Petrescu has never been a player to allow himself to be restricted to a single role. He is often seen assuming a striker's position in the opponents' penalty area and is quite happy to be his team's most advanced player. Combining defensive duties with a constant desire to push forward towards his opponent's goalmouth, he is responsible for many a final incisive pass that sets up a teammate with a goalscoring opportunity. And, although he is more a provider than a goalscorer, he is also a collected finisher who can calmly chip a keeper or slot the ball inside the far post. Petrescu can be relied upon to get more than his fair share of goals over the course of a season and is frequently on the score-sheet for Romania.

He captained the Steaua team that won the Romanian league four times before deciding to follow the exodus of great Romanian players. Since leaving his home country, he has never, until he signed for Chelsea, looked likely to add to his trophy room. He played in Italy for two unfashionable mid-table sides and his £1.25m move to England did little at first to revolutionize his fortunes. He never properly settled at Sheffield Wednesday and coach David Pleat was happy to let him go for £2.3m. This move to Chelsea was the turning point for the Romanian, however, as he won his first honour since leaving Bucharest, the English FA Cup in 1997.

The London team owes a lot to their Romanian wing-back for that triumph. Petrescu was the inspiration of the team that came back from 2–0 down to knock out Liverpool 4–2. He did his job well that day, eliminating Liverpool's attacks down the left flank before moving infield towards the end of the game and directing the kill as a support striker.

Petrescu missed Italia 90 through injury and so cannot be blamed for his team's failure at that tournament. It is no coincidence, however, that he was an ever-present in the rather more respectable campaign of USA 94. He is playing outstandingly well for Chelsea under Ruud Gullit and has been an inspiration to his international teammates in the run-up to France 98.

FULL NAME:	Daniele Vasile Petrescu
BORN:	22.12.67
BIRTHPLACE:	Bucharest
HEIGHT:	1.77m/5ft 10in
WEIGHT:	70kg/11st
CLUBS:	Steaua Bucharest, Foggia, Genoa, Sheffield Wednesday, Chelsea
DEBUT:	1989

❝ I want to play for a club with ambition and ability. ❞
— *Dan Petrescu on leaving Sheffield Wednesday*

DID YOU KNOW?
Petrescu played against his current club coach Ruud Gullit in the 1989 European Cup final. Gullit's Milan won 4–0.

THIS PAGE: DAN PETRESCU — A TOP CLASS DEFENDER AND ONE OF THE BEST PLAYERS IN THE WORLD WHEN HE COMES FORWARD INTO ATTACK.

OPPOSITE PAGE: IT'S HARD WORK PUTTING EIGHT GOALS PAST LIECHTENSTEIN.

The best example of the leaps and bounds that have been made in United States soccer over the past decade is the emergence of a young utility player from North Carolina called Eddie Pope. What may surprise many people around the world this summer is that the DC United prodigy's footballing brain has been exclusively developed in his home country. Yet this entirely home-grown talent is undoubtedly well up to the level of basic quality that will be required in France.

Such is his footballing ability that he can play pretty much anywhere in defence or in midfield, although he is most likely to appear on the right side of defence for the USA in France. His versatility has only recently been employed at international level, but he is already beginning to look like the team's best all-round player. He will almost certainly play if fit, and is definitely a major prospect for the future of United States soccer.

Unsurprisingly, Pope began his sporting career playing baseball and gridiron. But he also managed four years of football at the Southwest Guilford High School. At the University of North Carolina, where he began to take his football career seriously, he had been involved as a place kicker with a gridiron team. But his goalkicking exploits for the 'Tar Heels' (for whom he once recorded a 48-yard field goal) had not gone unnoticed by an increasing number of football coaches in that part of the world. Pope was soon persuaded to quit the indigenous code to concentrate on Association Football, as you'd expect any well-balanced individual to do given enough exposure to the beautiful game.

There are undoubtedly many great players yet to come out of a nation that has only recently begun to invest in its footballing stock, and there is nothing to say that the United States won't become a major challenger in World Cups to come, if not in France. But in the future, the name of Eddie Pope may well come to be remembered as the first player to convincingly prove that the MLS is a reputable factory of footballing talent.

FULL NAME:
Eddie Pope

BORN:
24.12.73

BIRTHPLACE:
Greensboro, NC

HEIGHT:
1.86m/6ft 1in

WEIGHT:
86kg/13st 8lbs

CLUBS:
DC United

DEBUT:
1996

❝ He's fair, he's clean, he's a gentleman. And he's also very effective. ❞
— DC United president Kevin Payne

DID YOU KNOW?
Pope was the first athlete in North Carolina to be invited to both the Association and American Football high school all-star games.

THIS PAGE: EDDIE POPE — HE HAS THE POTENTIAL TO BECOME THE BEST ALL-ROUND PLAYER THE USA HAS EVER PRODUCED.

OPPOSITE PAGE: THE DC UNITED STAR COULD BE CRUCIAL TO THE USA'S BID TO TAKE POINTS OFF GERMANY, YUGOSLAVIA AND IRAN TO GO THROUGH TO THE SECOND PLACE.

Romania
POPESCU

FULL NAME:
Georghe 'Gica' Popescu

BORN:
9.10.67

BIRTHPLACE:
Calafat

HEIGHT:
1.88m/6ft 2in

WEIGHT:
80kg/12st 8lbs

CLUBS:
University Craiova,
PSV Eindhoven,
Tottenham Hotspur, Barcelona

DEBUT:
1988

66 **His is the first name on the team-sheet.** 99
— *national coach Anghel Iordanescu*

DID YOU KNOW?
In qualifying, Popescu scored four times in one match against Liechtenstein.

THIS PAGE: GICA POPESCU — ROMANIA WILL NEED HIM ON TOP FORM IF THEY ARE TO CONTINUE THEIR WINNING WAYS IN FRANCE.

OPPOSITE PAGE: BATIGOL GETS THE BEST OF ROMANIA'S GICA POPESCU AT USA 94.

Like his fellow countryman Ilie Dumitrescu, 'Gica' Popescu never quite set the world on fire at Tottenham under Argentininian coach Osvaldo Ardiles. The team's poor run of form at that time was blamed on a negligence in their defensive duties and Popescu took much of the rap. He did his best to shore up the back line, but his style of football is so much the antithesis of the English game that he often seemed bemused by the lack of time he was allowed on the ball there. He remained in favour at White Hart Lane as long as Ardiles did, and no longer. When Gerry Francis took over at the North London club, Popescu, and Dumitrescu, were unceremoniously off-loaded. Nevertheless, English fans should not judge the abilities of the Romanian sweeper on this era alone.

A mark of the esteem in which this classy player is held throughout Europe is that he has twice been signed as a replacement for Holland's former international sweeper Ronald Koeman. It was Koeman's departure to Barcelona that prompted PSV Eindhoven to buy the Romanian from University Craiova, and when Koeman eventually hung up his boots at the Nou Camp, the man the Catalans bought to take his place was Gica Popescu.

Popescu is the player who makes it possible for gifted footballers like Georghe Hagi (see page 128) to show off their skills. He is the creator at the back, the man who strolls out of his own penalty area with the ball and seems to take an age to decide whom best to pass to. Though he may have struggled at Tottenham, he is never flustered at international level and is one of those footballers who is always capable of lifting his game for the big occasion.

This is Romania's third successive finals and their unbeaten run in qualification makes them an even more likely outside bet for the World Cup than ever before. Romania's daunting current form are both largely due to the calming influence of this now highly experienced attack-minded sweeper.

DEFENCE
Romania
PRODAN

R omania's most reliable stopper is a player who makes the job of his sweeper Gica Popescu (see page 212) a lot easier. He is an uncompromising tackler and an experienced tactician who serves Popescu well as his right-hand man. Prodan, always alert, always aware of the threat of the next attack, has been a mainstay of one of the most consistently tight defences in international football over the last four years.

Prodan plays in a much more conservative role for Romania than he does at club level, where his sheer height makes him a daunting proposition in both penalty areas. As well as his undoubted aerial ability, the big man shows great ball control and also has a thunderous shot, as Glasgow Rangers fans will remember – he scored against them with a cracking volley in the Champions League.

Prodan began his career as a Third Division left-back, a position he still occasionaly assumes when the situation demands. It was his current national coach, Anghel Iordanescu, who signed him for Steaua and converted him to the central role where he now plays for both club and country. He made an immediate impact in his new position at Steaua, winning four straight league titles at the Bucharest club. The first of these coincided with his promotion from the under-21s to the full national eleven. The last was coupled with the Romanian Cup for a memorable domestic double.

It is surprising that in a half century of caps for his country, Prodan has only ever scored once. Atletico Madrid fans would find that hard to believe. The lanky defender netted on his debut for the Madrid club in a 4–2 victory over Extremadura. Nowadays, Prodan is being increasingly encouraged to come forward for set-pieces at Atletico Madrid and, as a result, is starting to score goals on a regular basis in the Spanish League.

His form means he looks set to continue at the top level at least for the duration of the remaining three years of his contract to his new club. His newly acquired experience abroad should serve him well in France.

FULL NAME:
Daniel Claudiu Prodan

BORN:
23.3.72

BIRTHPLACE:
Bucharest

HEIGHT:
1.88m/6ft 2in

WEIGHT:
82kg/12st 13lbs

CLUBS:
Olympia Satu Mare,
Steaua Bucharest, Atletico Madrid

DEBUT:
1993

> 66 It was not necessary for us to have such a row just two months before the European championship finals in England. 99
> — *Daniel Prodan on match-rigging allegations in the Romanian League*

DID YOU KNOW?
At Satu Mare, Prodan is remembered by fans for dedicating more time to his passion for cars than to football.

THIS PAGE: DANIEL PRODAN — THE UNSUNG HERO OF THE ROMANIAN SQUAD IS A MAJOR FACTOR IN THE TEAM'S EXTRAORDINARY DEFENSIVE RECORD.

OPPOSITE PAGE: ROMANIA'S RELIABLE DEFENDER LAYS OFF A PASS ON THE WAY TO VICTORY OVER ARGENTINA AT USA 94.

South Africa
RADEBE

FULL NAME:
Lucas Radebe

BORN:
12.4.69

BIRTHPLACE:
Diepkloof

HEIGHT:
1.85/6ft 8in

WEIGHT:
73kg/11st 7lbs

CLUBS:
Wolves, Wanderers, ACL Birds,
Kaizer Chiefs, Leeds United

DEBUT:
1992

INTERNATIONAL HONOURS:
African Nations Cup winner 1996

**66 Making it to the World Cup
finals is one of the greatest
feelings I'll ever have. 99**
— *Lucas Radebe*

DID YOU KNOW?
Radebe had never heard of Leeds
until he signed for them.

THIS PAGE: LUCAS RADEBE — A TRULY
WORLD CLASS PLAYER WHO WAS LEFT OUT
OF THE LEEDS UNITED TEAM FOR TOO LONG.

OPPOSITE PAGE: GOING UP FOR A BICYCLE
KICK UNDER THE ATTENTIONS OF TUNISIA'S
MEHDI BEN SLIMANE.

A cool, calm and collected defender whose reliability at the back is a perfect counter-point to the marauding cavalier style of his defensive partner Mark Fish (see page 185). Radebe is both an agile and composed marker who was considered South Africa's most skilful export when he left to sign for Leeds United. Although at first he had limited opportunity to play in England, he is now getting regular Premiership experience and believes he is playing the best football of his life there.

He was first spotted by Kaizer Chiefs while playing for a local side in a regional tournament and was promptly offered a contract by the Johannesburg giants. He has said he was initially apprehensive about leaving his hometown for the big city, but within two years he had been spotted by the then Leeds manager Howard Wilkinson and found himself preparing to emigrate to Yorkshire.

He had never previously thought he'd play in England, believing that if he was to play abroad at all it would be in Turkey or Switzerland. Nevertheless, he moved to England with compatriot Phil Masinga, (who has since moved on to play for Bari in Italy), but became frustrated when he lost his place in the side as he felt he was doing everything he could to prove himself. For a while he contemplated going back home but a change of management at Elland Road saved his Leeds career. He says that when George Graham took over, he gave every player a chance to prove their worth and the South African captain is now back as an integral part of the team.

As a realist he recognizes the extent of his team's inexperience. 'We had to learn the rudiments of the international game after such a long period of isolation in a very short space of time.' The *Bafana Bafana* had learned just enough to win the African Nations Cup after favourites and defending champions Nigeria had withdrawn. But whether Radebe will be able to cope with the world's best remains to be seen.

'GUARDIOLA' SALA

Guardiola Sala is a deep-lying midfielder whose job is the same as it always has been, to take the ball from the defence and distribute it to the strikers. Unlike his two Catalan compatriots, he very rarely gets involved in any attacks himself, preferring to sit back and hold position in the centre-circle where he has the best chance of retrieving the ball should the attack break down.

'Pep' Guardiola was one of three young Catalans who came to prominence in the Barcelona team in 1991 under former coach Johan Cruyff. The other two are Albert Ferrer and Sergi Barjuan. Between them they helped lift Barcelona to four consecutive League Championships, and all three still play for Barcelona. All three will also be in the Spanish squad for France 98.

El noi (the boy) has been vociferous in his criticism of the number of foreigners playing domestic football in Spain, once complaining of not being able to understand anything that was said in the changing room at Barcelona. Guardiola's own first language is Catalan, the mother tongue he shares with teammates Ferrer and Sergi. But his Castilian is up to scratch and anyway, the way he plays requires little understanding of the language he speaks. He rarely shouts as much as many people who play in his position do, preferring to let the ball do the talking.

Although he plays very deep, he is more of an attacking player than a defender in his mentality. He is never the one to organize the defence, and is not expected to chase back with every attacker who goes past him. Guardiola lets his defenders do those jobs while he saves his energy for when they get the ball back and he is given it in his own half. From there he has the skill and vision to spray his perfect passes around the pitch. Opposition coaches who recognize the importance of the role he plays in Spain's team might be inclined to push a defensive midfielder up to track him throughout the game.

FULL NAME:	Josep Guardiola Sala
BORN:	18.1.71
BIRTHPLACE:	Santpedor
HEIGHT:	1.83m/6ft
WEIGHT:	77kg/12st 2lbs
CLUBS:	Barcelona
DEBUT:	1991

> ❝ The injury to Guardiola limited the creative play of Barcelona. ❞
> — *Spanish football press*

DID YOU KNOW?
Guardiola Sala has been at Barcelona since 1984.

THIS PAGE: 'PEP' GUARDIOLA SALA — CELEBRATING A GOAL AGAINST YUGOSLAVIA IN THE CRUCIAL QUALIFIER.

OPPOSITE PAGE: BARCELONA AND SPAIN'S ANCHORMAN KNOWS HE'S IN THE WORLD CUP.

Germany
SAMMER

Germany's ginger-haired sweeper is without doubt their most important player and the pivot of all their defensive and attacking options. The German team plays a tried and tested system that all their opponents know and have come to expect, but that very few of them can actually deal with. Players stick to a strict formation, even when switching positions, and the opposition is given no room to manoeuvre inside the German half. Sammer marshals this formation. When they win the ball, they rarely risk losing it again in an over-ambitious counter-attack, preferring to keep possession and analyze the weak points in the other team, probing forward only when there is an option that promises a route to goal. Sammer directs this operation too.

He never takes any risks, rarely wandering far from his own penalty area and only ever crossing the halfway line to change ends and take penalties. According to statistical evidence compiled at Euro 96 and analyzed by researchers at Liverpool's John Moore University, his most frequent tactic is to bring right wing-back Stefan Freund into play with a short ball to his feet. When this option is not available to him, he will sometimes try a sweeping pass towards the left corner flag. So say the researchers.

Whether or not this is strictly true, and whether the intelligent conductor of the German team still plays the same way, and whether anyone can stop him anyway, remains to be seen. What is sure is that his creativity at the back is what makes the German team work.

Sammer would probably have played at Italia 90 had he been eligible. As it was, he was born in East Germany and so had to wait until a unified German team took on Switzerland after the World Cup. He was the only member of the East German team whose international prospects did not crumble with the Berlin Wall. As well as being a member of the victorious 1996 team, he has won the German League three times and the German Super Cup twice. His talents have been recognized in being made the German Player of the Year in 1995 and 1996 and the European Footballer of the Year in 1997. He may yet be as good as Franz Beckenbauer (see page 169).

FULL NAME:
Matthias Sammer

BORN:
5.9.67

BIRTHPLACE:
Dresden

HEIGHT:
1.81m/5ft 11in

WEIGHT:
75kg/11st 11lbs

CLUBS:
Dynamo Dresden, VfB Stuttgart, Inter Milan, Borussia Dortmund

DEBUT:
1990

INTERNATIONAL HONOURS:
European Championships winner 1996

> **Sammer has always been a key player for my team because he gives 100% in every match.**
> — *national coach Berti Vogts*

DID YOU KNOW?
Sammer was out of the team at the start of this season after a cartilage operation.

THIS PAGE: MATTHIAS SAMMER — GERMANY'S KEY PLAYER WILL HAVE TO BE STOPPED IF THE FAVOURITES ARE NOT TO WIN THEIR FOURTH TITLE.

OPPOSITE PAGE: REPRESENTING GERMANY AGAINST BOLIVIA AT USA 94.

Argentina
SENSINI

FULL NAME:
Roberto Nestor Sensini

BORN:
12.10.66

BIRTHPLACE:
Arroyo Seco

HEIGHT:
1.78m/5ft 10in

WEIGHT:
75kg/11st 11lbs

CLUBS:
Newell's Old Boys, Udinese, Parma

DEBUT:
1989

INTERNATIONAL HONOURS:
Copa America winner 1991

One player in the Argentinian set-up who knows the ropes in World Cup football is their highly regarded, but often controversial defender Roberto Sensini. The hardman at the back is a veteran of that dour Argentinian team that reached the World Cup Final in 1990.

This vast experience has turned Sensini into a much more versatile player who can play anywhere at the back and looks very strong coming forward with the ball. He now says that 'it makes no difference' to him whether he plays as a stopper or as a sweeper. 'Roberto Ayala (see page 174) and I complement each other well. He'll go up field and I'll stay back, or the other way round. It's not a problem. Though, in principle, Passarella prefers me to go forward and Ayala to stay back.'

The opposition might come to prefer that latter arrangement too. Sensini is an uncompromising tackler. He has an immense will to win, and his role in the team, by its very nature, involves the risk of picking up some bookings. If a player gets the better of him, he will often resort to illegal methods to prevent a direct attack on his goal. He is almost bound to incur the wrath of some country's supporters during the World Cup.

Over the years, he has also sometimes come under a lot of criticism in Argentina for occasionally erratic performances, but he is now recognized as a crucial old hand in this new-look Argentina team. And the team's results are starting to win over the support of the Argentinian people. Sensini says the build up to France 98 has 'given the whole team confidence and has improved their football'. But he also believes that Argentina have yet to reach their full potential. That may yet be to their advantage. They will have a full month together before the World Cup in which to reach the level of team understanding where they can achieve their own high expectations in France.

❝ The objective is to be first. ❞
— Roberto Sensini

DID YOU KNOW?
Sensini was one of Argentina's over-age players in the under-20 World Cup.

THIS PAGE: ROBERTO SENSINI — A REGULAR AT THE BACK FOR ARGENTINA SINCE ITALY 90.

OPPOSITE PAGE: THE HARD MAN AT THE BACK WHO LOVES TO GET FORWARD INTO ATTACK.

DEFENCE
Nigeria
UCHE

FULL NAME:
Okechukwu Alozie Uche

BORN:
27.09.67

BIRTHPLACE:
Lagos

HEIGHT:
1.92m/6ft 4in

WEIGHT:
90kg/14st 2lbs

CLUBS:
Go Ahead Eagles, Brondby,
Fenerbahçe

INTERNATIONAL HONOURS:
African Nations Cup winner 1994

The Nigerian squad features several familiar faces from USA 94, but the 'Gentle Giant' is one of their more experienced players. Indeed, for all the flair and inventiveness of the men in front of him, the great improvements in Nigerian football over the 1990s have been largely built around this rock-solid defender.

His sheer height makes him very difficult to beat in the air and he takes responsibility at the back for heading out any hopeful high balls and crosses. As a marker, he shows good agility in staying close to the wiliest of attackers, and although he perhaps isn't as quick as he was, his experience allows him to stand off his man a little and use his size to stop the forward getting past him. That he has never become a household name may be because he has never played for one of Europe's glamour clubs. But a good showing from Nigeria in France might earn him deserved global recognition as one of the best stoppers in football today.

After learning his trade with the ever-struggling Go Ahead Eagles in Holland and the more successful but equally unglamorous Brondby in Denmark, the 'Gentle Giant' has now played four seasons for Turkish giants Fenerbahçe in Eastern Istanbul, where his adopted name is Abdulkerim Rahim Uche. He has since been joined by international teammate 'Jay Jay' Okocha (see page 151) and is as important to the Turkish club's current run of good fortunes as he is to the Nigerian national side's continued success.

As well as being the kingpin of the defence, Uche will also come forward for set-pieces where he is always a great danger. He was an essential part of Nigeria's gold-medal winning Olympic team, and his influence was used to keep the Nigerians calm after it was feared for a while that their suspension from the Confederation Africaine de Football for human rights violations in the country would be extended to FIFA and that they would not be allowed to take their place in France.

66 **Our world class players such as Okechukwu Uche are indeed capable of bringing the World Cup to Nigeria.** 99
— *article in the Ajuba Mirror, Nigeria*

DID YOU KNOW?
Uche received a cheque for $10,000 when he scored Fenerbahçe's 2,000th league goal.

THIS PAGE: UCHE OKECHUKWU — ONE OF THE WORLD'S BEST CENTRAL DEFENDERS WHO COULD LEAD NIGERIA TO AFRICA'S FIRST EVER WORLD CUP.

OPPOSITE PAGE: THIS COMMANDING PRESENCE IN THE NIGERIAN DEFENCE DOES HIS JOB AGAINST SAUDI ARABIA.

FULL NAME:
Christian Ziege

BORN:
1.2.72

BIRTHPLACE:
Berlin

HEIGHT:
1.86m/6ft 1in

WEIGHT:
73kg/11st 7lbs

CLUBS:
Hertha Berlin, Zehtendorf Berlin, TSV Rudow, Südstern 08 Berlin, Bayern Munich, AC Milan

DEBUT:
1993

INTERNATIONAL HONOURS:
European Championships winner 1996

66 Although I was pleased with the way I performed in England, our success was down to the efforts of our squad as a whole. **99**
— Christian Ziege

DID YOU KNOW?
AC Milan signed Ziege on a free transfer.

THIS PAGE: CHRISTIAN ZIEGE — HAD HIS HAIR DONE SPECIALLY FOR THE VITAL HOME DRAW THAT SAW GERMANY THROUGH AT THE EXPENSE OF PORTUGAL LAST SEPTEMBER.

OPPOSITE PAGE: PLAYING THE BALL UP THE LINE WITH THE MINIMUM OF FUSS.

The penetrating runs this left-sided wing-back makes down the flank give Germany extra attacking options on that side and are the source of many a goalscoring opportunity. He is a tireless runner who covers a tremendous amount of ground during a game, and is also good enough on the ball to be able to look up early and spot a teammate making a promising run into the penalty area. These attacking talents, combined with constant reminders from Matthias Sammer (see page 221) to never forget his defensive responsibilities, have established this Bundesliga and UEFA Cup winner in the German side in over 30 full international games.

Germany expects a lot from its left-backs. In the 1974, 1978 and 1982 World Cups, Paul Breitner was good enough never to be overshadowed by any of his teammates, while Andreas Brehme was widely recognized as the best in the world when he eventually took over for 1986 and 1990. Christian Ziege is the 1990s version and no poor imitation. He doesn't have the shot of Breitner, nor the skill of Brehme, but he has the determination of both. He played at USA 94 and is currently learning a lot at AC Milan where he plays in his usual position, while former left-back Paolo Maldini (see page 198) has taken over Franco Baresi's (see page 168) role as the sweeper. The transformation is having limited success. For all their great players, Milan can't stop leaking goals.

That experience may affect the confidence of the German at international level, as might the three goals conceded to Albania that nearly cost the Germans qualification in their final qualifying match, but coach Berti Vogts is unlikely to make changes while the team continues to get results. This doesn't look the best team Germany have put out for years, but then they never do. Ziege is a proven international who was excellent in England at Euro 96 and the Germans are not known for letting in soft goals at the World Cup Finals.

NAME:
Gyula Grosics

COUNTRY:
Hungary

WORLD CUPS:
1954, 1958, 1962

Combined impeccable goalkeeping with the ability to act as an extra defender. When he retired, Hungarian football suffered.

NAME:
Lev Ivanovich Yashin

COUNTRY:
USSR

WORLD CUPS:
1958, 1962, 1966

A peerless shot-stopper who saved over 150 penalties in his career. The 40-year-old 'Black Panther' as he was nicknamed travelled with the Mexico 70 squad.

NAME:
Dino Zoff

COUNTRY:
Italy

WORLD CUPS:
1974, 1978, 1982

Unbeaten for over 1,000 minutes of football before West Germany 74, Zoff controlled Italy's notoriously efficient defence.

NAME:
Pat Jennings

COUNTRY:
Northern Ireland

WORLD CUPS:
1982, 1986

A great leader who took his country to two successive World Cups and was still their indomitable captain at the age of 40.

NAME:
Thomas Ravelli

COUNTRY:
Sweden

WORLD CUPS:
1990, 1994

Orchestrated and inspired the semi-finalists of four years ago. In both 1990 and 1994, Ravelli's domination of the penalty area was unequalled. He will be missed in France 98.

TACTICAL INNOVATIONS

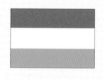

THE KEEPER/SWEEPER
**Pushed Up 3-5-2
with goalkeeper advancing out of the penalty area to sweep behind three defenders and two wing-backs**

With goalkeepers no longer allowed to pick the ball up from a back-pass, many are developing the ball-playing skills of the great Gyula Grosics to augment the defence. Denmark's Peter Schmeichel (see page 244) is an adept, while Colombia's Rene Higuita (see page 11, villains: Italy 90) patently isn't.

THE GREATEST

NAME:	
Gordon Banks	

COUNTRY:
England

BORN:
20.12.37

BIRTHPLACE:
Sheffield

WORLD CUPS:
1966-70

CAPS:
73

MOMENT OF GLORY

'Banks of England' was always known to his teammates as 'the world's greatest'. He proved that this was no idle acclaim with one incredible save in the intense heat of Guadalajara in 1970. England, the holders, faced Brazil, the hot favourites, in a first round match that many considered to be 'the final that never was'. Jairzinho had skinned left-back Terry Cooper and crossed from the bye-line for Pelé (see page 13) to lose his marker Alan Mullery and jump to head the ball down hard inside the near post. But as Pelé turned to celebrate his goal, Banks dropped like a stone to push the ball over the bar with one hand. Pelé later called it 'the greatest save I ever saw'.

After two World Cups and 17 years of domestic football for Chesterfield, Leicester and Stoke, Banks tragically lost the sight of an eye in a car crash. But he continued to play in the USA although he later said: 'I felt like a circus act when I was playing in America: roll up, roll up, roll up to see the greatest one-eyed goalkeeper in the world.'

Keeper moves forward to sweeper position while wingbacks and defenders move forwards.

GOALKEEPER

Paraguay
CHILAVERT

FULL NAME:
José Luis Chilavert Gonzalez

BORN:
27.7.65

BIRTHPLACE:
Tucumán

HEIGHT:
1.87m/6ft 1in

WEIGHT:
81kg/12st 11lbs

CLUBS:
Luquenyo, Velez Sarsfield

DEBUT:
1987

❝ If they want war, they shall have war. ❞
— Chilavert to Ecuador before the two countries met in qualification

DID YOU KNOW?
Uruguayan newspaper El Pais have made him their South American 'Dream Team' goalkeeper every year since 1995.

THIS PAGE: JOSÉ LUIS CHILAVERT — PARAGUAY'S INFLUENTIAL CAPTAIN AND GOALKEEPER.

OPPOSITE PAGE: WILL THE CAPTAIN SCORE A GOAL IN FRANCE? IT COULD BE WORTH AN OUTSIDER'S BET.

Argentinian-born goalkeeper José Luis Chilavert Gonzalez – or 'Chilavert', as he is perhaps best known – is far and away Paraguay's most famous player, and their most infamous. His skill between the sticks has made him a folk hero, not only in Paraguay but also in Argentina. The Argentinians love him for his performances in the Velez Sarsfield goal, but revile him for playing his international football for neighbours Paraguay, when he could have played for Argentina.

But Chilavert is Paraguayan and proud of it. His fellow countrymen are too, although their tempers must wear a little thin sometimes. The patience of the fans was tested nearly to its limits when Chilavert, their national team captain, received a six-match suspension last summer after assaulting Colombia's Faustino Asprilla (see page 18) in qualification. But the limit was extended when the fiery character was given a suspended prison sentence for attacking a rival team's trainer! There is no question, however, that he has also been the best goalkeeper in South America, at least since Colombia's Rene Higuita was in his prime.

Paraguay have shown that they can get results without their goalkeeper, but he is a talisman for the side and they play a lot more confidently with him behind them. Questioned last year on what he thought of Brazil's chances of defeating Paraguay, he admitted that he thought they had a good team but that what interested him most was 'Paraguay, a team of intelligent footballers who are ready to give their all for their country on the field tomorrow'. That's fighting talk and Chilavert is famous for it.

He is also famous for taking his team's penalties, but his goalscoring armoury doesn't end there. Nor is it just a case of him coming forward for last ditch attacks like Denmark's Peter Schmeichel (see page 244). In one season in Argentina, Chilavert scored from open play against Boca Juniors, Olimpia and River Plate – that last one from the halfway line. He has won everything at club level with Velez Sarsfield and is constantly being showered with accolades as the best player in Paraguay, the best in Argentina, in America and in the world. Now's his chance to show that to be true.

Safe hands that are exceptionally good at dealing with crosses have made this good basketball player an even better goalkeeper. He is also an intimidating prospect for any striker as he races out to cut down the angles. So much so that many teams at France would like to have him in their squad. There is fierce competition for the USA's Number One jersey, but Brad Friedel's claim to it is that he has averaged over one clean sheet for every four games. Having kept another shut-out as the USA defeated Canada 3–0 last November to ensure their qualification for France, Friedel currently finds himself just ahead of Kasey Keller and Jürgen Sommer in the pecking order. But he has only recently been promoted to first choice and he will need to maintain the superb form he has shown for Columbus Crew if he is to stay there for the duration of the World Cup finals.

Friedel is another player who has come through the ranks of college and Olympic football. He had played both tennis and basketball, as well as football, for his high school, but went to UCLA as a goalkeeper. There he won the Hermann Trophy in 1993, the award for the best college player in the United States. He had played in the victorious Pan-American team of 1991 and for the Olympic team in 1992, and was already recognized as one of the country's top goalkeepers. He first came to Europe in 1994 for trials with Newcastle United in the English Premiership, but his work permit was not granted. He returned to the English north east the following year, but was denied the opportunity Sunderland were prepared to offer him as his career was again foiled by the British government. He was accepted in Denmark, however and gained some vital European experience at Brondby.

After returning to the USA to play for Columbus Crew, his claim for a British work permit was again initially refused. But the British Government eventually relented and the keeper signed for Liverpool in December as a possible replacement for the off-form David James.

FULL NAME:
Brad Friedel
BORN:
18.5.71
BIRTHPLACE:
Lakewood, OH
HEIGHT:
1.93m/6ft 4in
WEIGHT:
92kg/14st 7lbs
CLUBS:
Brondby, Galatasaray, Columbus Crew, Liverpool
DEBUT:
1993

66 I think Brad, for sure, is one of the top 10 goalkeepers in the world. **99**
— Columbus Crew coach Tom Fitzgerald

DID YOU KNOW?
Friedel was the MLS 1997 Goalkeeper of the Year.

THIS PAGE: BRAD FRIEDEL — HAS HE COME TO PROMINENCE AS THE USA NUMBER ONE GOALKEEPER AT JUST THE RIGHT TIME?

OPPOSITE PAGE: BRAD FRIEDEL BEHAVING RATHER STRANGELY IN A FRIENDLY AGAINST BELGIUM IN 1995.

Germany
KOEPKE

Right at the very back of tightest defence in world football is a man who seems to be getting an easy ride. Although they say there are 'no easy games in international football', there are games where your grandmother could keep goal for the Germans, such is the infrequency with which the opposition gets a shot on goal. With world class defenders like Matthias Sammer and Jürgen Kohler (see pages 221 and 194) playing in front of him, Köpke rarely gets anything to do. But whenever he is called into action, even if it is only once in an entire game, he shows that he has been concentrating all along by pulling off some great and vital saves.

The penalty he stopped from England's Gareth Southgate in the semi-final shoot-out that defeated the hosts of the 1996 European Championships and sent Germany to the final was not the best he's ever made, but it was perhaps the most important. It put Germany through to Wembley where Köpke won his first major international tournament. Of all the German team in England that summer, Köpke was one of the players who most deserved the victory. He showed his class throughout the tournament, keeping clean sheets against both Italy and Russia in successive matches, and his assuredess and composure were very important to Germany's success. He was linked with moves to Stuttgart and also to Barcelona after the tournament but chose to go to Marseille where he is currently helping the beleaguered club back to greatness.

That he is so rarely called upon to perform heroics is as much a credit to his own discipline in keeping the defence in shape as it is to the efforts of his sweeper Sammer. Yet he still has to look over his shoulder for two other great keepers who are looking to take his place in the national team. Bodo Illgner and Oliver Kahn will both probably also be part of the German squad for France 98, and both be hoping to claim their place in the team in the unlikely event that national coach Berti Vogts decides to make any late changes.

FULL NAME:
Andreas Köpke

BORN:
12.3.62

BIRTHPLACE:
Kiel

HEIGHT:
1.82m/6ft

WEIGHT:
80kg/12st 8lbs

CLUBS:
Eintracht Frankfurt, Marseille

DEBUT:
1990

INTERNATIONAL HONOURS:
European Championships winner 1996

❝ **The world's best goalkeeper currently playing.** ❞
— *The Federation of International Statisticians*

DID YOU KNOW?
Köpke knocked Italy out of Euro 96 with a penalty save in normal time from Gianfranco Zola (see page 93)

THIS PAGE: ANDREAS KOEPKE — THE KEEPER BELLOWS OUT HIS INSTRUCTIONS TO HIS DEFENDERS.

OPPOSITE PAGE: STARTING ANOTHER GERMAN COUNTER-ATTACK AGAINST PORTUGAL IN QUALIFYING.

GOALKEEPER
Austria
KONSEL

FULL NAME:
Michael Konsel

BORN:
6.3.62

BIRTHPLACE:

HEIGHT:
1.85m/6ft 1in

WEIGHT:
78kg/12st 4lbs

CLUBS:
Austria Vienna, Rapid Vienna, Roma

DEBUT:
1990

66 Whenever many Austrians play for foreign clubs, our national team is always strong. **99**
— *coach Herbert Prohaska after Konsel's transfer from Rapid to Roma*

DID YOU KNOW?
Konsel is a survivor of the Rapid Vienna side that lost to Everton in the 1985 Cup-Winners' Cup Final.

THIS PAGE: MICHAEL KONSEL — DESPITE FIERCE COMPETITION, HE LOOKS IN POLE POSITION FOR AUSTRIA'S NUMBER 1 SHIRT IN FRANCE.

OPPOSITE PAGE: AUSTRIA'S ROCK-SOLID DEFENCE IS CONTROLLED BY THIS DEPENDABLE VETERAN.

M ichael Konsel is a veteran goalkeeper discovering a new lease of life in Serie A after 13 seasons and over 400 appearances for Rapid Vienna. Roma coach Zdenek Zemen picked up Austria's first-choice goalkeeper in 1997 in order to plug the leaky defence that cost the club a place in Europe in 1997/98. And Konsel's form repaid Zemen's faith as a series of impressive clean-sheets kept the sleeping Stadio Olimpico giants among the early pace-setters.

Konsel made his League debut for Austria Vienna back in 1984, but played just a handful of games before switching to the city's premier club, Rapid, in February 1985. There, he carried off Austrian Bundesliga titles in 1987 and 1988, as well as a brace of Austrian cup winners' medals, before international recognition arrived in 1990. He was given the chance to earn the right to replace Tirol's Klaus Linderberger after Austria's disappointing World Cup in Italy. Superb reflexes and a tremendous command of his area made him a great favourite of coach Alfred Riedl, but after some shaky performances in his country's doomed USA 94 qualification campaign, Konsel lost his place to Austria Vienna's Franz Wohlfahrt.

Under the present coach, legendary Herbert Prohaska, Konsel reclaimed the keeper's jersey, only to give a nightmare performance against Northern Ireland, when Austria were thumped 5–3 in soggy Belfast. That result cost his side qualification for Euro 96 and Austria's other international-standard goalkeepers began to come back into the picture. Undeterred, Konsel bounced back to pick up a third Bundesliga medal with Rapid. He was also able to retain his national shirt, despite immense pressure from Real Zaragoza goalie Otto Konrad. His record in qualifying for France speaks for itself. In nine World Cup qualifiers, Konsel conceded just four goals, two of which were scored at Celtic Park by Scotland's Kevin Gallacher (see page 37) in Austria's only defeat. Austria will need their keeper to show similarly consistent form in France. Konsel has the extra incentive of knowing that there are people on the bench perfectly capable of taking his place if he should falter.

GOALKEEPER
Scotland
LEIGHTON

With their young bandy-legged keeper shutting out the opposition, Aberdeen were a major force in both Scottish and European football in the early 1980s. The consistently excellent performances of Scotland's most promising goalkeeper in living memory had also elevated Jim Leighton into the international squad as back-up for first-choice keeper Alan Rough.

Leighton first took over from Alan Rough in the Scotland goal shortly after Spain 82 and then played throughout the qualifying matches for Mexico 86 and in the finals themselves. Although Scotland went home after the first round without winning a game, Leighton was not held responsible for their early exit and he kept his place in the team. By the time he joined Manchester United in 1988, it was beginning to look like Scotland had at last found a truly world-class goalkeeper.

Then it all began to go horribly wrong. The safest hands in Scotland started to make a series of incomprehensible mistakes that first cost the keeper his confidence and then his place in both the Manchester United and Scotland teams. One error in the World Cup qualifier against Norway nearly cost his country their place at Italia 90 and after a disastrous experience in the FA Cup Final, a further mistake against Brazil was enough to see Scotland out of the tournament.

He was replaced as Manchester United keeper and spent three years out of the national team until being recalled to World Cup action as a replacement for the injured Andy Goram for a qualifier against Malta. Three years on, he is first choice again. In qualifying for France 98, it was Jim Leighton's form that shut the Swedes out until just before half-time. In the return match, he was outstanding as the Scots secured the 1-0 win that eventually proved the edge over their group rivals.

Up until the end of qualifying, Leighton was averaging a clean sheet for every two of his nearly 80 caps. That is a commendable record, but Scotland will need him to be at his best in France. They are hoping that their quiet keeper's confidence will hold at least until the end of the World Cup.

FULL NAME:
Jim Leighton

BORN:
24.7.62

BIRTHPLACE:
Johnstone

HEIGHT:
1.86m/6ft 1in

WEIGHT:
78kg/12st 4lbs

CLUBS:
Aberdeen, Manchester United, Hibernian, Aberdeen

DEBUT:
1983

66 **I benefit now from all the experience, my fitness is good and my age doesn't come into it.** 99
— Jim Leighton

DID YOU KNOW?
Leighton won the European Cup Winners' Cup with Aberdeen in 1983, defeating Real Madrid 2–1 in the final.

THIS PAGE: JIM LEIGHTON — FOR A WHILE HE WAS AWFUL, BUT AT HIS BEST HE'S AWESOME. AND HE'S RETURNING TO HIS BEST.

OPPOSITE PAGE: SCOTLAND'S JIM LEIGHTON BACK IN THE TEAM FOR THE VITAL WORLD CUP QUALIFYING VICTORY OVER SWEDEN

Italy
PERUZZI

T he Italians had the hardest run-in to their qualification programme imaginable. A buoyant England claimed a draw in Rome to take first place in their group and the Italians had to travel to Moscow to thrash out a 1–1 draw in freezing temperatures against a Russian team whose wide play would have given most teams nightmares at France 98. The Italians won the return match 1–0 to qualify. Their goalkeeper for the second of those games was Angelo Peruzzi and, unless he makes any nasty mistakes before the tournament, he is likely to remain coach Arrigo Sacchi's first choice. But the Juventus man has a lot of competition for his place.

Angelo Peruzzi has ten years of Serie A experience. At the age of just 17, he made his league debut for Roma away to AC Milan. To play at the San Siro is as big an occasion as there is in Italian football, but the young keeper kept a clean sheet as Roma came away with a 2–0 win. It was to be his only first-team game that season however, and it wasn't until he spent the 1989/90 season as a Verona player that he gained some regular team experience. He returned to his original club for one more year before signing for Juventus in 1991. But Peruzzi would have to wait another year before he became the team's first choice. Since then he has been a regular for the Turin club.

His position in the Italian side is not so stable. Peruzzi was injured in training during the Euro 96 qualifiers and Francesco Toldo came in to the side to have a great game against Croatia in Split after original replacement Luca Bucci had been sent off early in the game. But Peruzzi kept his place as first choice for the finals in England. However, he has also recently had to contend with Gianluca Pagliuca's claim to the Italian goalkeeper's shirt. As the country's strenuous qualification for France came to a close, it was the Juventus man who was just ahead of his rivals in Coach Arrigo Sacchi's plans.

FULL NAME:
Angelo Peruzzi

BORN:
16.2.70

BIRTHPLACE:
Viterbo

HEIGHT:
1.81m/5ft 11in

WEIGHT:
88kg/13st 12lbs

CLUBS:
Roma, Verona, Juventus

DEBUT:
1995

❝ We have played too many games and we haven't improved. ❞
— *Angelo Peruzzi after losing to England at Le Tournoi*

DID YOU KNOW?
Angelo Peruzzi became a father for the first time in March 1996.

THIS PAGE: ANGELO PERUZZI — HIS FORM AT BOTH CLUB AND INTERNATIONAL LEVEL IS KEEPING THE JUVE MAN JUST AHEAD OF PAGLIUCA AS ITALY'S FIRST-CHOICE KEEPER.

OPPOSITE PAGE: STRONG PERFORMANCES FROM THE GOALKEEPER AGAINST ENGLAND AND RUSSIA HELPED ITALY SQUEEZE THROUGH TO THE FINALS.

Mexico
RIOS

Although he has been selected to play for Mexico by the last three national coaches, Adolfo Rios, despite his unquestionable abilities, has hitherto always been kept on the fringes of the team by the Mexican goalkeeping legend Jorge Campos. But with Campos now at the end of his international career and playing out the rest of his days in the MLS for LA Galaxy, Adolfo Rios is beginning to get a regular run in the Mexican national team.

He is not the tallest of goalkeepers but his agility and extraordinary reflexes make him an excellent shot-stopper, and if he plays in the multi-coloured dreamcoat that seems to be becoming the traditional attire of Mexico's goalkeepers, his flamboyant style may well make him one of the great characters of France 98, should Mexico live up to expectations by making it through their first-round group.

Taking over from his predecessor was never going to be easy for the new incumbent, but his performances in qualifying have meant that Adolfo Rios has now firmly made a name for himself as the country's number one keeper and, having played in Mexico's victorious USA Cup team of 1997, the year in which he also kept goal for the side that reached third place in the Copa America, he is almost certain to be the first choice in France.

Rios began his career for UNAM in 1986 and made his international debut in February 1987 in a 2–1 friendly international victory against Portuguese club side Sporting Lisbon. At club level, he helped the 'Pumas' to the runners-up spot in the Mexican League in 1988 before signing for Veracruz in 1990, where he reached the final of the Mexican Cup in 1995, and was voted Mexican Goalkeeper of the Year in 1997. He was transferred to Necaxa in 1997, where he has joined international teammate Garcia Aspe (see page 97). There he may well be given the opportunity to play against his predecessor in the Mexican goal, as Necaxa have a recent history of playing friendly matches against LA Galaxy.

FULL NAME:
Jose Adolfo Rios Garcia

BORN:
11.12.66

BIRTHPLACE:
Uruapan

HEIGHT:
1.76m/5ft 9in

WEIGHT:
71kg/11st 3lbs

CLUBS:
UNAM, CD Veracruz, Necaxa

DEBUT:
1987

> **66** He is an excellent goalkeeper who is giving his best to the team. **99**
> — *former Mexican keeper Jorge Campos*

DID YOU KNOW?
Rios saved three penalties against Ecuador in a shoot-out at the last Copa America.

THIS PAGE: ADOLFO RIOS – A TREMENDOUS ATHLETE WHO IS LIKELY TO BE KEPT VERY BUSY IN FRANCE.

OPPOSITE PAGE: JORGE CAMPOS IS A TOUGH ACT TO FOLLOW, BUT RIOS HAS FILLED THE LEGEND'S BOOTS WELL.

Denmark
SCHMEICHEL

W idely recognized as the best goalkeeper in the world today, Peter Schmeichel has been Denmark's first-choice keeper for a decade. Over that time, he has collected a century of international caps and, at the age of 34, shows no signs of giving up the Number One jersey.

Beginning his career as a youth player under former national coach Richard Moller-Nielsen, he went on to make over 200 appearances for Brondby in three years there before moving to Old Trafford in 1991 for £500,000. A year later, he was the rock upon which the Danes built their 1992 European Championship victory.

Peter Schmeichel has won four League Championships and the FA Cup with Manchester United, and is their most consistent performer. His absence from the team was noted after he suffered a back injury against Crystal Palace in November 1994. The Red Devils were comprehensively beaten by both Barcelona and Gothenborg in the European Cup and also lost their unbeaten home record in the league. Their fortunes did not improve until Schmeichel was fit again.

He is a dominating presence in goal, extremely fast off his line, and he uses his size well to cut down angles. For his defenders, he is domineering, always shouting, always organizing and never allowing his players to slacken off. But the other facet of his game that makes him so important to his team is the way he can transform defence into attack with his enormous throw. He has also been known to come forward for last-minute corners and free-kicks whenever his team needs a late goal. One such foray resulted in a fine headed goal against Rotor Volgograd in the UEFA Cup.

Schmeichel met his match at Euro 96, however. Davor Suker (see page 85) found a way to lift the ball over the big keeper to complete a resounding victory for Croatia. But after that disappointing defence of their title, Danish coach Bo Johansson showed confidence in Schmeichel by making him team captain for the assault on the World Cup.

FULL NAME:
Peter Bolesaw Schmeichel

BORN:
18.11.63

BIRTHPLACE:
Glodsone

HEIGHT:
1.96m/6ft 5in

WEIGHT:
89kg/14st

CLUBS:
Gladsaxe, Hbidovre IF, Brondby, Manchester United

DEBUT:
1987

INTERNATIONAL HONOURS:
European Championship winner 1992

❝ Every country would like Peter Schmeichel as their goalkeeper. ❞
— *former national coach Richard Moller-Nielsen*

DID YOU KNOW?
Schmeichel was given odds of 25/1 to score against Everton in the 1994 FA Cup Final.

THIS PAGE: PETER SCHMEICHEL — QUITE PROBABLY THE BEST GOALKEEPER IN THE WORLD.

OPPOSITE PAGE: WAS GORDON BANKS THE BEST EVER? OR WAS IT LEV YASHIN? OR IS IT THIS MAN, DENMARK'S PETER SCHMEICHEL?

GOALKEEPER
England
SEAMAN

When Peter Shilton vacated the yellow of the England goalkeeper's jersey, his understudy 'Spunky' was only one of several pretenders to the by now multi-coloured garment. Seaman has been described as looking like a packet of sweets at England matches as the goalkeeper's kit went through a period of artistic licence. But the confidence and ease he has shown at international level, not least at Euro 96, means that the likes of Nigel Martyn and David James will now have to miss the fancy dress party while the Arsenal keeper takes the stage for his first World Cup.

Seaman will always be notorious for making the crucial mistake of coming too far off his line in the last minute of the 1995 European Cup Winners' Cup Final, allowing Zaragoza's Nayim to lob him from the halfway line. However, it should be remembered that he had played in the team that had won that same trophy the previous season and also that he has now won all England's domestic honours with Arsenal.

After being rejected by Leeds as a teenager, the prospect of his becoming a baker's apprentice rather than a professional goalkeeper ended when he was offered a chance to prove himself at Peterborough. He gladly accepted that opportunity before eventually signing for Arsenal in 1990. At Highbury, with his England teammate Tony Adams (see page 170) playing in front of him, he has been at the back of the country's stingiest club defence ever since.

Seaman didn't appear at Italia 90 and never played for England under Graham Taylor, but his international career spans ten years and that experience shows in his ruthless command of the penalty area. This softly spoken Yorkshireman, who wouldn't say boo to a goose off the pitch, is a dominating goalkeeper who marshals his defence with authority, hardly ever misses the crosses he chooses to come out for and also has the lightning reflexes necessary to make great saves. In fact, he shows no obvious weaknesses at all and has been consistently playing at the top of his game for some years now. With him guarding the net, England will be very hard to score against.

FULL NAME:
David Seaman

BORN:
19.9.63

BIRTHPLACE:
Rotherham

HEIGHT:
1.93m/6ft 4in

WEIGHT:
93kg/14st 10lbs

CLUBS:
Peterborough United, Birmingham City, QPR, Arsenal

DEBUT:
1988

66 **The worst thing about being a goalkeeper is the fear of making a big mistake.** 99
— *David Seaman*

DID YOU KNOW?
Seaman rates Peter Shilton as England's greatest ever keeper.

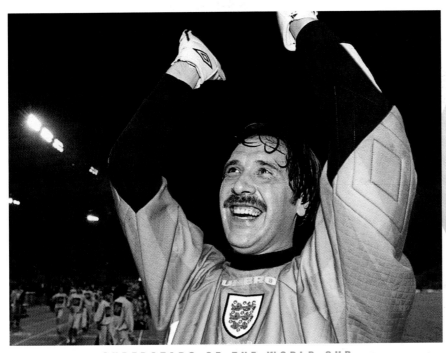

THIS PAGE: DAVID SEAMAN — APPLAUDING THE FANS AFTER ENSURING QUALIFICATION IN ROME.

OPPOSITE PAGE: CALLING FOR DEFENSIVE COVER AGAINST THE EVER DANGEROUS ITALIANS.

Cameroon
SONGO'O

It is part of a goalkeeper's lot that there is only room for one player in that position on the team. And for a long time, Cameroon's current captain, Jacques Songo'o, sat on the bench as his international career was eclipsed by the fame and adulation surrounding fellow goalkeepers Thomas Nkono and Joseph-Antoine Bell.

Songo'o was part of the Cameroon squad for both Italia 90 and USA 94 but has only ever made one appearance at the tournament. And it wasn't the game he would have chosen. The unfortunate keeper was hardly to blame for the 6–1 defeat by a rampant Russia in 1994; a result like that never does much to further any goalkeeper's career. Nevertheless, after 15 years in and out of the team, Songo'o has now become recognized as the nation's automatic first-choice goalkeeper and looks almost certain to reach the 100 caps mark for his country.

Songo'o left his homeland for Toulon after Italia 90. He was on the French club's books for four years, but failed to make much of an impression and played the last of those seasons on loan to Le Mans in the Second Division. He then signed for Metz, and his career started to blossom. He was a key part of that club's improving fortunes during his time there, and had begun to develop into the composed and intelligent keeper who has stood behind the tight Deportivo defence since 1995. He will almost certainly keep goal for Cameroon in France.

Songo'o played in both the qualifiers and the finals of the 1997 African Nations Cup, but was helpless to prevent his country's surprise first-round exit at the hands of South Africa and Egypt. In his first World Cup as a firm choice for the team, the new captain will try to prove that Cameroon's failure to make an impact in Burkina Faso last year was no more than a blip on the chart of their rise to dominance in African football in the 1990s.

FULL NAME:
Jacques Celestin Songo'o

BORN:
17.3.64

BIRTHPLACE:
Sakbayanne

HEIGHT:
1.82m/5ft 7in

WEIGHT:
80kg/12st 8lbs

CLUBS:
Canon Yaounde,
Tonnerre Yaounde, Toulon,
Le Mans, Metz,
Deportivo La Coruña

DEBUT:
1983

INTERNATIONAL HONOURS:
African Nations Cup winner 1988

> 66 He called me 'black'...he lacked respect for me. 99
> — *Jacques Songo'o on Spain's Fernando Hierro*
> *(see page 157)*

(see page 157)

DID YOU KNOW?
Songo'o was voted best keeper in Spain in 1996.

THIS PAGE: JACQUES SONGO'O – CAMEROON WILL NEED HIS EXPERIENCE AND CLASS IN FRANCE.

OPPOSITE PAGE: THE GREAT GOALKEEPER VOICES HIS OPINION.

South Korea
SOO

Q uick off his line and an excellent shot-stopper, South Korean goalkeeper Kim Bong Soo is a tall and dominating presence at the back for the Asians. Although he has yet to ensure his place in the first team for France 98, he has looked more than impressive recently, and now that qualification for the finals has been ensured once again, Kim Bong Soo looks their most likely choice for the Number One jersey. Kim Bong Soo had won only 14 international caps by the end of the qualification phase for France 98. Despite making his debut almost a decade ago against Iran, just one week after his 18th birthday, he has previously had to play second fiddle to the likes of Oh Yun Kyo, Choi In Yong, and more recently, Kim Byung Ji. But he played in two of four games in Korea's first round of qualifying against Thailand and Hong Kong, and regularly in the second round. It is unlikely that the Koreans will want to make too many changes to an increasingly successful team that made light work of their qualification programme.

Indeed, South Korea are Asia's most successful team ever at World Cup level. France 98 will be their fifth appearance, and will also mark their fourth successive finals. As joint hosts with Japan for the World Cup in 2002, they will automatically qualify, thereby achieving a recent World Cup record that will be the envy of almost every other country.

While the Japanese, the Korean Republic's co-hosts for the World Cup finals in four years time, will be happy just to make an appearance in France, their neighbours now feel that they are reaching a level where they can compete with the Africans, Europeans and the South Americans. You will probably still hear a lot of nonsense about their supposed lack of physical presence, but with Kim Bong Soo in goal, the Korean defence rarely has too much difficulty in dealing with long, high balls into the box, and the rest of the team can play a bit too.

FULL NAME:
Kim Bong Soo

BORN:
4.12.70

BIRTHPLACE:
Seoul

HEIGHT:
1.85m/6ft 1in

WEIGHT:
76k/12st

CLUBS:
Anyang LG Cheetahs

DEBUT:
1988

66 With Kim Bong Soo in goal, the Korean defence rarely has too much difficulty in dealing with long, high balls into the box. 99

DID YOU KNOW?
Kim Bong Soo scored against Thailand in qualifying for France.

THIS PAGE: KIM BONG SOO — CAN THE GOALKEEPER KEEP THE CLEAN SHEETS THAT WILL TAKE KOREA PAST THE GROUP STAGE?

OPPOSITE PAGE: HE'S NOT THE ONLY KEEPER THE KOREANS HAVE AT THEIR DISPOSAL, BUT HE IS THE FORM MAN OF THE MOMENT.

GOALKEEPER
Romania
STELEA

D espite intense competition from other international-class keepers in the Romanian set-up, the shaven-headed Bogdan Stelea has kept goal for the national team in all but the first game of their unbeaten qualification programme. It is a measure of influence on the team that he is keeping the likes of Florin Prunea on the bench. However, the Romanian's second-choice keeper is still in contention and will be ready to take over if Stelea's performances become erratic and the team start to leak goals. This prospect is unlikely to unnerve the Romanian Number One. Rather, it is more probable that it will inspire him to the levels of vigilance he has often been accused of not attaining.

Perhaps it is the fact that Romania conceded only four goals in ten qualifying games that keeps Stelea ahead of the pack. On that sort of form, it is not surprising that he is the current first choice. But the much-travelled keeper would have played more than 40 times for his country had it not been for Silvio Lung and Florin Prunea. They both know that the current incumbent has been notorious for the kind of display he showed against France at Euro 96, but they also know that Stelea's record since that tournament speaks for itself.

Stelea first made his mark by winning the Romanian domestic Double with Dinamo Bucharest in 1990 and was soon sought after abroad. But having failed to win any trophies on his travels, he went home to win a second domestic double, this time with Steaua, before moving back to Spain. Like many of his compatriots, the goalkeeper is highly confident of Romania's chances of going all the way this time. 'We have so many class players and we will prove it in France,' he threatens. The first part of that claim is undeniable. Always one of Europe's stronger sides, Romania's daunting form made them the first European country to qualify for France 98; and nowhere are they stronger than in the goalkeeping department. This is likely to be Stelea's last World Cup and he is preparing for a great swan song.

FULL NAME:
Bogdan Stelea

BORN:
5.12.67

BIRTHPLACE:
Bazna

HEIGHT:
1.82m/5ft 7in

WEIGHT:
84kg/13st 2lbs

CLUBS:
Dinamo Bucharest, Mallorca, Standard Liege, Rapid Vienna, Samsunspor, Steaua Bucharest, Salamanca

DEBUT:
1989

66 In all my time in the national team, I've never been really sure of my place. 99
— Bogdan Stelea

DID YOU KNOW?
Stelea conceded and then saved a penalty from Eire's Roy Keane in qualifying.

THIS PAGE: BOGDAN STELEA — THE MAN CURRENTLY PLAYING BEHIND WORLD FOOTBALL'S BEST DEFENCE.

OPPOSITE PAGE: BOGDAN STELEA ROLLS THE BALL OUT FOR STEAUA BUCHAREST IN A 1995 PRE-SEASON FRIENDLY MATCH AGAINST GLASGOW RANGERS.

GOALKEEPER
Spain
ZUBIZARRETA

If the Basques formed a national team, they would take half the Spanish side with them and 'Zubi' would be the player the Castilians missed the most. After beginning his career in 1978 at Alaves, he first played for Atletico Bilbao in 1981. He won the Spanish league with them in 1983 and followed that up with the league and Cup Double in 1984. His consistency finally gave him his international debut in January 1985, and he has been Spain's first-choice keeper ever since. He has now been made team captain.

Spain went out of the 1986 and 1990 World Cups in penalty shoot-outs and were disposed of in the second phase of USA 94 by Yugoslavia after extra-time. Zubizarreta's four World Cup finals appearances are as much as anyone, including Pelé, has managed, and an all-time record fifth tournament at the age of 40 is highly unlikely, even for a player of his stature.

The £1m Barcelona paid for him in 1986 was, at that time, a world record price for a goalkeeper, but he proved himself well worth the investment over nearly a decade of service to the Catalan club, where he was always a favourite with supporters. In an international friendly match in 1987, he conceded four Gary Lineker goals as England beat Spain 4–2 in Madrid. That was bad enough, but Lineker was his teammate at Barcelona at the time and the Real Madrid fans duly noted the fact when the two clubs met in the league the next week. Lineker silenced them all with his second hat-trick in four days. The Catalans cheered Zubizarreta.

Many thought his international career was all but over when he was released by Barcelona and moved down the coast to Valencia. But although he had fallen out of favour with Johan Cruyff (see page 95) at the Nou Camp, he is still Spain's first-choice goalkeeper under Javier Clemente, who trusts in Zubi's tremendous influence on a team that has yet to fulfil its potential.

FULL NAME:
Andoni Zubizarreta

BORN:
23.10.61

BIRTHPLACE:
Vitoria

HEIGHT:
1.87m/6ft 2in

WEIGHT:
86kg/13st 8lbs

CLUBS:
Alaves, Athletic Bilbao, Barcelona, Valencia

DEBUT:
1985

66 He's still one of the best keepers in the world. 99
— national coach Javier Clemente

DID YOU KNOW?
Zubizarreta is Spain's most capped player ever.

THIS PAGE: ANDONI ZUBIZARRETA — IT'S BEGINNING TO LOOK LIKE HE'LL BE PLAYING GOAL FOR SPAIN FOREVER.

OPPOSITE PAGE: THAT LEFT FOOT CAN DROP A BALL ONTO A TEAMMATE'S CHEST FROM 60 METRES AWAY.

INDEX